MRCP 1
POCKET BOOK
2

Basic Sciences, Neurology, and Psychiatry

David W. Ray PhD MRCP
Edward Tobias MBChB MRCP PhD
Donal J. O'Donoghue BSc MBChB FRCP
Geraint Rees BM BCh MD MRCP PhD
Christopher E G Moore MRCP
M. Zoha MBChB MRCPsych
Richard S Hopkins MRCPsych

First edition 2002

ISBN: 1 901198 804

A catalogue record for this book is available from the British Library.

The information contained within this book was obtained by the author from reliable sources. However, while every effort has been made to ensure its accuracy, no responsibilty for loss, damage or injury occasioned to any person acting or refraining from action as a result of information contained herein can be accepted by the publishers or author.

Typeset by Breeze Limited, Manchester
Printed by MPG Books Limited, Bodmin, Cornwall

CONTENTS

INTRODUCTION

PasTest's MRCP Part 1 Pocket Books are designed to help the busy examination candidate to make the most of every opportunity to revise. With this little book in your pocket, it is the work of a moment to open it, choose a question, decide upon your answers and then check the answer. Revising 'on the run' in this manner is both reassuring (if your answer is correct) and stimulating (if you find any gaps in your knowledge).

For quite some time the Royal College of Physicians has been conducting an extensive review of the MRCP Part 1 examination and has recently announced changes to be introduced in May 2002. From an educational point of view both these changes are to be welcomed.

Negative marking (penalty scoring) will be discontinued
From the candidates' point of view, this is an important change because incorrect answers will no longer be penalised by the deduction of marks – they will simply not gain any marks. (From the Examiners' point of view it should improve the reliability of the examination by removing an uncontrollable variable – individual candidates' willingness to venture an answer when they are less than 100% confident.)

A second paper will be introduced in addition to the current 2½ hour, 60 question multiple true/false examination. This will also last for 2½ hours, but consist of 100 questions using a new type of Multiple Choice Question (MCQ) – the one-best answer/'Best of Five' format.
This means that the examination from May 2002 onwards will last all day. Candidates will also need to become familiar with one-best MCQs and the strategies for answering them. However, one-best is a much better design than multiple true/false. They are typically more valid and reliable, so their introduction should be to the advantage of good candidates.

One-best answer/'Best of Five' MCQs
An important characteristic of one-best answer MCQs is that they can be designed to test application of knowledge and clinical problem-solving rather than just the recall of facts. This should change (for the better) the ways in which candidates prepare for MRCP Part 1.

Each one-best MCQ has a question stem, which usually contains clinical information, followed by five branches. All five branches are typically homologous (e.g. all diagnoses, all laboratory investigations, all antibiotics etc) and should be set out in a logical order (e.g. alphabetical). Candidates are asked to select the ONE branch that is the best answer to the question. A response is not required to the other four branches. The answer sheet is, therefore, slightly different to that used for true/false MCQs.

A good strategy that can be used with many well-written one-best MCQs is to try to reach the correct answer without first scrutinising the five options. If you can then find the answer you have reached in the option list, then you are probably correct.

One-best answer MCQs are quicker to answer than multiple true/false MCQs because only one response is needed for each question. Even though the question stem for one-best answer MCQs is usually longer than for true/false questions, and therefore takes a little longer to read carefully, it is reasonable to set more one-best than true/false MCQs for the same exam duration – in this instance 60 true/false and 100 one-best are used in exams of 2 hours.

Application of Knowledge and Clinical Problem-Solving

Unlike true/false MCQs, which test mainly the recall of knowledge, one-best answer questions test application and problem-solving. This makes them more effective test items and is one of the reasons why testing time can be reduced. In order to answer these questions correctly, it is necessary to apply basic knowledge – not just be able to remember it. Furthermore, candidates who cannot reach the correct answer by applying their knowledge are much less likely to be able to choose the right answer by guessing than they were with true/false MCQs. This gives a big advantage to the best candidates, who have good knowledge and can apply it in clinical situations.

Multiple Choice Questions

Each question consists of an initial statement followed by five possible completions, ABCDE. There is no restriction on the number of true or false items in a question. It is possible for all items in a question to be true or for all to be false. The most important points of technique are:

1. Read the question carefully and be sure you understand it.
2. Mark your response clearly, correctly and accurately.
3. The best possible way to obtain a good mark is to have as wide a knowledge as possible of the topics being tested in the examination.

To get the best value from the MCQ sections you should commit yourself to an answer for each item before you check the correct answer. It is only by being sure of your own responses that you can ascertain which questions you would find difficult in the examination.

Books like the ones in this series, which consist of 'Best of Five' and MCQs in subject categories, can help you to focus on specific topics and to isolate your weaknesses. You should plan a revision timetable to help you spread your time evenly over the range of subjects likely to appear in the examination. PasTest's Essential Revision Notes for MRCP by P Kalra will provide you with essential notes on all aspects of the syllabus.

BASIC SCIENCES

'Best of Five'

David W. Ray PhD MRCP
Glaxo-Wellcome Research Fellow
and Honorary Consultant in Endocrinology
University of Manchester and Manchester Royal Infirmary
Manchester

Edward Tobias MBChB MRCP PhD
Glaxo-Wellcome Clinical Research Fellow
and Honorary Consultant in Medical Genetics
Department of Medical Genetics
University of Glasgow
Glasgow

MCQs

Donal J. O'Donoghue BSc MBChB FRCP
Consultant Renal Physician
Department of Renal Medicine
Hope Hospital
Salford

BASIC SCIENCES: 'BEST OF FIVE' QUESTIONS

For each of the questions select the ONE most appropriate answer from the options provided.

1.1 **Hormones are capable of acting at distant sites via specific, high affinity receptors. Concerning hormone action which one of the following statements is true?**

- ☐ A ACTH receptors are coupled to G proteins
- ☐ B Cortisol binds to the mineralocorticoid receptor
- ☐ C Insulin acts by causing dimerisation of two subunits of the insulin receptor, and stimulating adenylate cyclase
- ☐ D pARalpha binds to the thiazolidine group of drugs
- ☐ E Thyroid hormone binds to a membrane receptor

1.2 **In thyrotoxicosis, appropriate management depends on the aetiology, and associated pathologies**

- ☐ A Carbimazole is contraindicated in pregnancy
- ☐ B Graves' disease is associated with myasthenia gravis
- ☐ C Graves' ophthalmopathy requires high dose steroid treatment
- ☐ D Radioactive iodine improves exophthalmos in Graves' disease
- ☐ E Toxic multinodular goitre may go into long-term remission following a course of carbimazole

1.3 **The clinical diagnosis of adrenal insufficiency is suggested by which one of the following?**

- ☐ A Hypertension
- ☐ B Hypoglycaemia
- ☐ C Hypokalaemia
- ☐ D Neutrophilia
- ☐ E Pallor

1.4 **In the clinical evaluation of gynaecomastia which one of the following underlying diagnoses is unlikely?**

- ☐ A   Amiodarone
- ☐ B   Klinefelter's syndrome
- ☐ C   Renal failure
- ☐ D   Spironolactone
- ☐ E   Testicular malignancy

1.5 **In the management of acromegaly which one of the following statements is correct?**

- ☐ A   90% of patients respond to long acting somatostatin analogue treatment
- ☐ B   Diabetes mellitus occurs in <5% of patients
- ☐ C   Hypercholesterolaemia is common
- ☐ D   Patients with pituitary microadenomas can be cured in 50% of cases
- ☐ E   Suprasellar extension prevents a transsphenoidal surgical approach

1.6 **Concerning monoclonal antibodies which one of the following statements is NOT true?**

- ☐ A   They are being used to limit transplant rejection
- ☐ B   They are made using human B lymphocytes
- ☐ C   They can be used to activate T lymphocytes in vitro
- ☐ D   They can be used to detect proteins in histological sections
- ☐ E   They can be used to measure hormones in blood

1.7 **Which one of the following is a characteristic of mitochondrial diseases?**

- ☐ A   They cause hypothyroidism
- ☐ B   They cause ketoacidosis
- ☐ C   They cause 'ragged red' fibres in skeletal muscle
- ☐ D   They involve the renal tubule
- ☐ E   They are paternally inherited

1.8   Concerning genetic anticipation

☐   A   It is characteristic of neurofibromatosis type I

☐   B   It is not seen with fragile X syndrome

☐   C   It refers to earlier diagnosis due to improved awareness

☐   D   It occurs in Turner's syndrome

☐   E   It results from amplification of triplet repeats within genes

1.9   Concerning the regulation of gene expression which one of the following statements is correct?

☐   A   Introns are not transcribed into mRNA

☐   B   Mammalian mRNA tends to be polycistronic

☐   C   Mutations in the DNA sequence encoding a gene always result in changes in the amino acid sequence of the resulting protein

☐   D   RNA polymerase II gives rise to protein encoding mRNA

☐   E   The majority of cellular RNA is mRNA

1.10   Tumour necrosis factor alpha

☐   A   Activates the NFkB transcription factor

☐   B   Binds a single, specific receptor

☐   C   Inhibits expression of interleukin 1

☐   D   Is useful treatment for rheumatoid arthritis

☐   E   Leads to enhanced insulin sensitivity

1.11   In rheumatoid arthritis which one of the following is true?

☐   A   Association of seropositivity with HLA DR1

☐   B   Concordance rate of >60% for identical twins

☐   C   Peak incidence in the 3rd decade

☐   D   Progression from predominantly small peripheral joint disease to involve more proximal, larger joints

☐   E   Sacroiliac joint disease is common

1.12   In polymyalgia rheumatica

☐ A   EMG studies detect a typical abnormality

☐ B   Night sweats and fever make the diagnosis unlikely

☐ C   One half of patients are aged less than 60 years

☐ D   Patients have a characteristic reduction in circulating CD8+ T lymphocytes

☐ E   The response to prednisolone is helpful in diagnosis

1.13   The HLA B27 molecule is

☐ A   A class II major histocompatibility antigen

☐ B   Expressed on antigen presenting dendritic cells

☐ C   Found in 50% of Caucasians with ankylosing spondylitis

☐ D   Over-represented in Crohn's disease

☐ E   Over-represented in Whipple's disease

1.14   Vasculitis may be due to different disease processes. Which one of the following statements is NOT true?

☐ A   Antibodies to proteinase 3 are specific for vasculitis

☐ B   Churg-Strauss syndrome patients typically present with asthma

☐ C   Polyarteritis nodosa mainly affects small vessels

☐ D   There is a seasonal peak in incidence in North America

☐ E   Wegener's granulomatosis affects the small vessels of the kidney

1.15   SLE is a systemic inflammatory disease. Which one of the following statements is true concerning SLE?

☐ A   15% have Raynaud's phenomenon

☐ B   C reactive protein is a useful marker of disease activity

☐ C   Decreased incidence in Klinefelter's syndrome

☐ D   High frequencies of disease are seen in women of Chinese ancestry

☐ E   Skin is affected in <50% of cases

1.16 **Concerning urinary sediment which one of the following is correct?**

- ☐ A <100 white cells per ml is normal
- ☐ B Cystine crystals are often found in normal urine
- ☐ C Hyaline casts consist of Tamm-Horsfall protein
- ☐ D Oxalate crystals in the urine suggest renal disease
- ☐ E Red cells always indicate renal tract disease

1.17 **Patients with renal failure may require drug treatment in addition to haemodialysis. Which one of the following drugs is dialysed by haemodialysis?**

- ☐ A Acyclovir
- ☐ B Erythromycin
- ☐ C Propranolol
- ☐ D Vancomycin
- ☐ E Warfarin

1.18 **In the evaluation of a patient with raised urea and creatinine, pre-renal failure is unlikely if there is**

- ☐ A Decreased pulmonary wedge pressure
- ☐ B Postural hypotension
- ☐ C Urine osmolality >500 mosm/l
- ☐ D Urine sodium >20 mmol/l
- ☐ E Urine to plasma urea ratio of >8

1.19 **Concerning adult polycystic kidney disease which one of the following is true?**

- ☐ A 10% of affected patients will also have hepatic cysts
- ☐ B Abdominal pain is a common presenting feature
- ☐ C Autosomal recessive inheritance
- ☐ D Generally results in end stage renal failure in the third decade
- ☐ E Spontaneous haematuria is unusual

1.20 **Concerning acid-base function of the kidney which one of the following statements is NOT true?**

☐ A >80% of all filtered bicarbonate ions are actively recovered

☐ B In distal renal tubular acidosis (RTA type I) there is normal anion gap, metabolic acidosis and urinary pH >5.5

☐ C Nephrocalcinosis suggests type I or distal RTA

☐ D Proximal renal tubular acidosis is usually an inherited condition

☐ E The proximal nephron actively secretes hydrogen ions, in contrast to the distal nephron

1.21 **With regard to human immunodeficiency virus (HIV)**

☐ A CD8 cells become depleted as disease progresses

☐ B HIV 1 and HIV 2 are closely related, and cause similar disease progression

☐ C HIV gains entry to the cell via the TNF receptor

☐ D It is a lentivirus

☐ E The HIV genome contains circular DNA

1.22 **Concerning pneumococcal disease**

☐ A Pneumococcal meningitis is associated with similar mortality rates to meningococcal meningitis in industrialised countries

☐ B Pneumococcal otitis media is usually associated with neutrophil leukocytosis

☐ C Pneumococcal pneumonia has no seasonal variation in temperate countries

☐ D *Pneumococcus* is a Gram-negative organism

☐ E Sickle cell disease predisposes to pneumococcal infection, and antibiotic prophylaxis is ineffective

1.23 **Concerning herpes simplex virus infection which one of the following is correct?**

☐ A 10% of herpes encephalitis cases are due to reactivation of virus

☐ B Antibody titres are helpful in making management decisions

☐ C Is caused by a single stranded DNA virus

☐ D Meningitis is a relatively benign condition in adults

☐ E Precedes 50% of all cases of erythema multiforme

1.24 **Concerning meningococcal disease which one of the following statements is untrue?**

☐ A Haemorrhagic skin lesions are a late feature of septicaemia

☐ B Identification of Gram-positive diplococci on lumbar puncture suggests meningococcal meningitis

☐ C Meningococcaemia is associated with neutrophilia

☐ D Rifampicin eradicates nasal carriage in less than 30% of contacts

☐ E Transmission is usually by respiratory droplet

1.25 **Fever in a patient returning from foreign travel is unlikely to be due to typhoid fever if which one of the following clinical features is present?**

☐ A Altered mental state

☐ B Associated headache

☐ C Change in bowel habit

☐ D Haematuria

☐ E There is no diurnal variation in the temperature

1.26 **Which one of the following is true of Marfan's syndrome?**

☐ A Aortic dissection is a recognised complication

☐ B Mutations in the collagen gene are typical

☐ C New mutations in the gene are rare

☐ D The inheritance pattern is X-linked dominant

☐ E The mutations generally occur at the same position within the gene

1.27 **Blood vessel rupture is not a recognised complication of which one of the following genetic conditions?**

☐ A Ehlers-Danlos syndrome

☐ B Marfan's syndrome

☐ C Polycystic kidney disease

☐ D Pseudoxanthoma elasticum

☐ E Velocardiofacial syndrome

1.28 **In Klinefelter's syndrome, which one of the following is correct?**

- ☐ A   Severe learning difficulties are common
- ☐ B   Significant gynaecomastia is present in almost all cases
- ☐ C   The incidence is about 1 in 50,000 new-born males
- ☐ D   There is a 10–15% chance of recurrence of a chromosomal abnormality after the birth of a child with Klinefelter's syndrome
- ☐ E   There is no increase in the incidence of homosexuality

1.29 **Which one of the following conditions is correctly paired with a gene responsible for that condition?**

- ☐ A   Achondroplasia   *SMN* (survival motor neurone)
- ☐ B   Congenital muscular dystrophy   *sarcoglycans*
- ☐ C   HNPCC   *hMLH1*
- ☐ D   Limb-girdle muscular dystrophy   *merosin*
- ☐ E   Spinal muscular atrophy   *FGFR3*

1.30 **Which one of the following is true of nuclear DNA?**

- ☐ A   Approximately 97% codes for proteins
- ☐ B   Base-pairing is mediated by covalent bonds
- ☐ C   Coding sequences are interrupted by non-coding exons
- ☐ D   It exists predominantly as a nucleoprotein complex
- ☐ E   Sugar and phosphate molecules are linked together by hydrogen bonds

BASIC SCIENCES: MULTIPLE CHOICE QUESTIONS

Mark your answers with a tick (True) or a cross (False) in the box provided.

1.31   In the cardiac cycle

☐ A   isovolumetric contraction occurs after the 2nd heart sound

☐ B   the venous C wave occurs during ventricular contraction

☐ C   the rate of ventricular filling increases throughout diastole

☐ D   mean left ventricular pressure equals mean aortic pressure

☐ E   during inspiration ventricular ejection is prolonged

1.32   3–hydroxy–3–methyl glutaryl–CoA (HMGCoA) reductase inhibitors

☐ A   can cause gout

☐ B   increase HDL cholesterol

☐ C   preferentially reduce triglycerides

☐ D   can cause myositis

☐ E   increase insulin sensitivity

1.33   Losartan

☐ A   is a specific renal angiotensin converting enzyme inhibitor

☐ B   induces cough in only approximately 5% of patients

☐ C   can be used safely in renal artery stenosis

☐ D   may exacerbate hyperkalaemia

☐ E   reduces angiotensin II levels in the efferent renal arteriole

1.34   Cystic fibrosis

☐ A   phenotype correlates with cystic fibrosis transmembrane regulator function

☐ B   is associated with obstructive azoospermia

☐ C   results from a single mutation to the cystic fibrosis transmembrane conductance regulator gene

☐ D   is inherited in an autosomal dominant fashion

☐ E   can be excluded if genotyping is normal

1.35   Physiological factors that increase the P50 of haemoglobin – O$_2$ include

- ☐ A   increase in hydrogen ion concentration
- ☐ B   reduction in pCO$_2$
- ☐ C   increase in temperature
- ☐ D   increase in 2,3 diphosphoglycerate (2,3 DPG)
- ☐ E   reduced chloride ion concentration

1.36   Allergic bronchopulmonary aspergillosis

- ☐ A   is associated with eosinophilia
- ☐ B   usually occurs in patients with chronic asthma
- ☐ C   antibodies to *Aspergillus* can be detected in serum
- ☐ D   *Aspergillus* antigen skin testing is rarely positive
- ☐ E   is a form of extrinsic allergic alveolitis

1.37   Factor V Leiden

- ☐ A   results in enhanced sensitivity to protein C
- ☐ B   occurs due to a premature stop codon in the gene for factor V
- ☐ C   venous thromboembolic risk is only increased in homozygotes
- ☐ D   is an acquired defect
- ☐ E   is associated with recurrent abortion

1.38   Vitamin B12

- ☐ A   is absorbed in the ileum
- ☐ B   requirements are increased in lead poisoning
- ☐ C   is a co-enzyme in red cell membrane synthesis
- ☐ D   is transported by intrinsic factor to the bone marrow
- ☐ E   deficiency is associated with gastric carcinoid formation

1.39   Glucose-6-phosphate dehydrogenase deficiency

- ☐ A   is an autosomal recessive condition
- ☐ B   provides protection against *Plasmodium falciparum*
- ☐ C   haemolysis can be precipitated by chloroquine
- ☐ D   haemoglobin electrophoresis is normal
- ☐ E   results in osmotic fragility

1.40 **The following cause resistance to erythropoietin treatment of renal anaemia:**

- ☐ A   iron deficiency
- ☐ B   infection
- ☐ C   antibodies to erythropoietin
- ☐ D   hyperparathyroidism
- ☐ E   angiotensin converting enzyme inhibitors

1.41 **The following drugs accumulate if renal function is impaired:**

- ☐ A   tobramycin
- ☐ B   simvastatin
- ☐ C   acyclovir
- ☐ D   allopurinol
- ☐ E   nifedipine

1.42 **Low dose (renal dose) dopamine**

- ☐ A   improves renal perfusion in healthy humans
- ☐ B   results in a natriuresis
- ☐ C   improves renal function in established acute renal failure
- ☐ D   can be associated with bowel ischaemia
- ☐ E   does not result in arrhythmias

1.43 **The following may enhance the oral hypoglycaemic action of sulphonylureas:**

- ☐ A   trimethoprim
- ☐ B   bendrofluazide
- ☐ C   rifampicin
- ☐ D   bezafibrate
- ☐ E   alcohol

1.44 The following are causes of hyperprolactinaemia:

- [ ] A ranitidine
- [ ] B thyroxine
- [ ] C methyldopa
- [ ] D oestrogens
- [ ] E haloperidol

1.45 Adrenal insufficiency

- [ ] A can be precipitated by rifampicin
- [ ] B requires treatment with high dose steroids
- [ ] C does not require treatment with fludrocortisone
- [ ] D circulating adrenal antibodies occur in over 70%
- [ ] E can be associated with spastic paralysis in females

1.46 Hereditary angioedema

- [ ] A is inherited as a sex linked condition
- [ ] B can present with abdominal pain
- [ ] C is due to a deficiency in the C1q component of complement
- [ ] D results in low C2 and C4 complement components in plasma
- [ ] E responds to danazol treatment

1.47 Type IV hypersensitivity

- [ ] A involves mast cell degranulation
- [ ] B occurs in contact dermatitis
- [ ] C is initiated by antibody
- [ ] D can result in granulomatous reactions
- [ ] E is a feature of myasthenia gravis

1.48 Rheumatoid factors

- [ ] A are typically IgM antibodies
- [ ] B bind the Fab fragment of IgG
- [ ] C include antinuclear antibodies
- [ ] D are present in the synovial fluid in rheumatoid arthritis
- [ ] E are acute phase reactants

1.49   Internuclear ophthalmoplegia

☐   A   results in failure of abduction of the eye ipsilateral to the lesion

☐   B   when caused by lesions of the right side, causes nystagmus on abduction of the left eye

☐   C   results from a lesion in the centre for lateral gaze

☐   D   does not affect vertical gaze

☐   E   causes dilation of the ipsilateral pupil

1.50   In multiple sclerosis

☐   A   saltatory conduction is impaired

☐   B   MHC class II expression is increased in the CNS

☐   C   the blood–brain barrier is intact

☐   D   oligodendrocytes are unaffected

☐   E   helper T cells are found in acute lesions

1.51   Anti-acetylcholine antibodies

☐   A   are typically IgM isotype

☐   B   can result from penicillamine treatment

☐   C   are polyclonal

☐   D   may arise as a paraneoplastic phenomenon

☐   E   are not complement fixing

1.52   The following vaccines should be avoided in immunocompromised patients:

☐   A   diphtheria

☐   B   BCG

☐   C   hepatitis B

☐   D   tetanus

☐   E   pneumococcus

1.53   In schistosomiasis

☐ A   risk of infection is related to fresh water exposure

☐ B   nephrotic syndrome is a late sequelae

☐ C   adult schistosomes multiply with a doubling rate of 28 days in the human host

☐ D   eosinophilia does not occur

☐ E   treatment with praziquantel should be continued for 6 weeks

1.54   *Borrelia burgdorferi*

☐ A   is a spirochaete

☐ B   causes babesiosis

☐ C   characteristically causes erythema migrans

☐ D   is resistant to penicillins

☐ E   is Gram negative

1.55   Alpha interferon treatment of hepatitis B

☐ A   is most effective in patients with normal transaminase levels

☐ B   results in long term remission in 80% of patients

☐ C   is ineffective if there is coincidental hepatitis D infection

☐ D   increases the risk of bacterial infections

☐ E   frequently results in transient increases in transaminase levels

1.56   Hepatitis C

☐ A   is a DNA virus

☐ B   is a more frequent cause of chronic viral hepatitis than hepatitis B

☐ C   often results in markedly elevated transaminases with only minor histological changes

☐ D   does not respond to alpha interferon

☐ E   can result in cryoglobulinaemic mesangiocapillary glomerulonephritis

1.57   Intestinal fat absorption

☐   A   requires bile salt acids

☐   B   occurs predominantly in the terminal ileum

☐   C   requires pancreatic amylase

☐   D   is inhibited by neomycin

☐   E   requires a functional LDL receptor

1.58   The complement system

☐   A   can only be activated by immunoglobulins

☐   B   involves a cascade of proteins resulting in formation of the membrane attack complex

☐   C   is involved in tissue injury in lupus nephritis

☐   D   is controlled by membrane bound proteins that inactivate the terminal complement components

☐   E   is defective in paroxsymal nocturnal haemoglobinuria

1.59   Mitochondrial DNA

☐   A   is single stranded

☐   B   abnormalities are associated with diabetes mellitus

☐   C   is paternally inherited

☐   D   consists of 23 molecules per mitochondria

☐   E   mutates more frequently than nuclear DNA

1.60   The polymerase chain reaction

☐   A   produces multiple copies of DNA

☐   B   occurs at 40°C

☐   C   requires oligonucleotide primers

☐   D   can be used to detect functional polymorphisms

☐   E   is of high specifity but low sensitivity

NEUROLOGY

'Best of Five'

Geraint Rees BM BCh MD MRCP PhD

Wellcome Advanced Fellow
Institute of Neurology
University College
London

MCQs

Christopher E G Moore MRCP

MRC Training Fellow and
Honorary Senior Registrar
Manchester Royal Infirmary
Manchester

NEUROLOGY: 'BEST OF FIVE' QUESTIONS

For each of the questions select the ONE most appropriate answer from the options provided.

2.1   **A 43-year-old woman complains of unsteadiness, syncope, constipation and urinary retention. She was previously well, takes no medications and has no relevant family history. On physical examination you find bradykinesia, mild resting tremor, and severe postural hypotension. Which one of the following is the MOST likely diagnosis?**

☐   A   Huntington's chorea

☐   B   Idiopathic Parkinson's disease

☐   C   Multiple system atrophy

☐   D   Normal pressure hydrocephalus

☐   E   Progressive supranuclear palsy

2.2   **A 56-year-old man with poorly controlled diabetes complains of horizontal diplopia. You notice a subtle convergent strabismus. His diplopia is worse on looking to the right, and on covering his right eye he tells you that the outer image disappears. Which one of the following cranial nerves is the MOST likely site of the underlying lesion?**

☐   A   Left abducens nerve

☐   B   Left oculomotor nerve

☐   C   Right abducens nerve

☐   D   Right oculomotor nerve

☐   E   Right trochlear nerve

2.3   A 58-year-old woman is brought to A&E unresponsive after collapsing at her home. Her husband reports that she felt well that morning, but developed a progressively severe headache. She has a history of hypertension and atrial fibrillation for which she is anticoagulated. On examination she has a blood pressure of 220/140 mmHg and has apnoea alternating with hyperpnoea. She responds only to noxious stimuli with right-sided extensor posturing. She has papilloedema and an unreactive pupil on the left, diffuse hyperreflexia and bilateral upgoing plantars. Which one of the following herniation syndromes is MOST consistent with her clinical presentation?

☐ A   Brain stem through the tentorial notch
☐ B   Cerebellar tonsils through the foramen magnum
☐ C   Cingulate gyrus beneath the falx
☐ D   Diencephalon through the tentorial notch
☐ E   Temporal lobe uncus across the tentorium

2.4   A 62-year-old man develops left-sided limb ataxia, Horner's syndrome, nystagmus and loss of pain and temperature sensation on his face. The MOST likely cause is occlusion of which one of the following arteries?

☐ A   Basilar artery
☐ B   Posterior cerebral artery
☐ C   Posterior inferior cerebellar artery
☐ D   Superior cerebellar artery
☐ E   Vertebral artery

2.5   A 31-year-old man gives a three-year history of increasing deafness and tinnitus in his right ear. He is a smoker and has no other medical history. On examination, his auditory acuity is grossly impaired on the left. Rinne's test shows air conduction greater than bone conduction. You notice no nystagmus, and balance is normal, but the left corneal reflex is absent. Which one of the following is the MOST likely diagnosis?

☐ A   Acoustic neuroma
☐ B   Basilar artery aneurysm
☐ C   Brainstem astrocytoma
☐ D   Multiple sclerosis
☐ E   Nasopharyngeal carcinoma

2.6   A 52-year-old woman presents with a three-month history of right-sided tingling, numbness and weakness. Her entire right side is completely numb, yet hypersensitive to touch. Five years earlier she underwent mastectomy for breast carcinoma. You find a hemiplegic gait, right hemianaesthesia to all sensory modalities, minimal weakness and flexor plantars. Which one of the following is MOST likely to be causing these symptoms and signs?

- [ ] A   Left posterior cerebral artery infarction
- [ ] B   Left postcentral gyrus metastasis
- [ ] C   Left thalamic metastasis
- [ ] D   Multiple sclerosis
- [ ] E   Right cerebellar infarction

2.7   A 26-year old man, previously healthy, complains of progressive visual loss accompanied by intermittent central headaches. On examination you note a bitemporal inferior quadrantanopia, but no other neurological abnormalities. Which one of the following diagnoses is MOST likely?

- [ ] A   Craniopharyngioma
- [ ] B   Cushing's disease
- [ ] C   Optic neuritis
- [ ] D   Prolactinoma
- [ ] E   Retinitis pigmentosa

2.8   A 48-year-old hypertensive man tripped while playing football, and awoke the next day with severe foot drop. On examination, foot eversion is impaired and there is there is severe weakness of dorsiflexion. The ankle reflex is intact, and there is no evidence for sensory loss. Which one of the following structures is MOST likely to be damaged?

- [ ] A   Common peroneal nerve
- [ ] B   Femoral nerve
- [ ] C   L5/S1 nerve root
- [ ] D   Sciatic nerve
- [ ] E   Tibial nerve

2.9 A 36-year-old Asian man presents with a two-day history of sore throat, headache and vomiting. Two years previously he underwent splenectomy following a road traffic accident. On examination, he is confused, disoriented, febrile and photophobic. He is tachycardic and you notice a petechial rash on his upper arms, together with mild neck stiffness and positive Kernig's sign. There is no papilloedema. Which one of the following is the diagnosis?

- [ ] A   Haemophilus meningitis
- [ ] B   Herpes simplex encephalitis
- [ ] C   Meningococcal meningitis
- [ ] D   Pneumococcal meningitis
- [ ] E   Tuberculous meningitis

2.10 A 76-year-old woman is brought to clinic by her daughter. She is worried about her mother's increasing forgetfulness. Her mother has had increasing difficulty managing at home over several months, forgetting what she has bought and getting lost while out at the shops. The presence of which one of the following abnormalities lends most weight to a diagnosis of Alzheimer's disease?

- [ ] A   Constructional apraxia
- [ ] B   Disinhibition
- [ ] C   Disorientation in time
- [ ] D   Episodic memory deficit
- [ ] E   Visual hallucinations

2.11 A 32-year-old woman presents with choreiform movements and intellectual decline over a period of several years. She denies any family history of neurological disorder. On examination she has continual choreiform jerks involving the hands and feet; sensation, power and reflexes are normal with flexor plantars. Which one of the following is the MOST likely diagnosis?

- [ ] A   Huntington's chorea
- [ ] B   Multiple sclerosis
- [ ] C   Neuroacanthocytosis
- [ ] D   Parkinson's disease
- [ ] E   Wilson's disease

2.12   A 68-year-old female smoker complains of progressive difficulty with writing and simple mental arithmetic. On examination you find a lower right homonymous quadrantanopia; neuropsychological testing confirms a mild dyscalculia, dysgraphia and finger agnosia. You order a MRI scan; damage to which one of the following structures do you suspect is responsible for her symptoms?

☐ A   Left frontal lobe

☐ B   Left occipital lobe

☐ C   Left parietal lobe

☐ D   Right parietal lobe

☐ E   Left temporal lobe

2.13   A 34-year-old woman presents complaining of episodic leg weakness and crampy abdominal pain without diarrhoea. During an episode, her abdomen is distended with decreased bowel sounds, and distal leg weakness with loss of knee and ankle jerks. These findings suggest a defect in the biosynthetic pathway for

☐ A   Collagen

☐ B   Corticosteroids

☐ C   Glucose

☐ D   Haeme

☐ E   Thyroxine

2.14   A 24-year-old man presents with a seven-day history of progressive lower limb paraesthesiae, numbness extending from both feet up to the lower abdomen, and difficulty walking. Numbness has started to develop in his hands. You find generalized weakness on examination and areflexia, but without definite sensory loss. Which one of the following is the MOST likely diagnosis?

☐ A   Cervical cord compression

☐ B   Guillain-Barré syndrome

☐ C   Motor neurone disease

☐ D   Myasthenia gravis

☐ E   Polymyositis

2.15 A 26-year-old woman presents with two episodes of loss of consciousness. On each occasion she remembers a strong smell immediately before losing consciousness. Her work colleagues who observed these episodes report that she sat motionless at her desk, chewing repetitively for a few seconds, before slumping forwards. She was unconscious for about thirty seconds; subsequently appearing confused and disoriented for a few minutes. Physical examination, EEG and MRI are all normal. Which one of the following treatments is likely to be MOST appropriate?

☐ A Carbamazepine

☐ B Ethosuximide

☐ C Gabapentin

☐ D Lamotrigine

☐ E Phenytoin

2.16 A 26-year-old woman is brought to the accident and emergency department having collapsed in a nightclub with a tonic-clonic seizure. When you see her, she is awake and complaining of nausea and headache. On examination she has moderate pyramidal weakness of the right leg. A CT scan shows bilateral haemorrhagic infarction of the white matter in the left parietal lobe. The MOST likely cause is occlusion of which one of the following blood vessels?

☐ A Cavernous sinus

☐ B Left middle cerebral artery

☐ C Left posterior cerebral artery

☐ D Right anterior cerebral artery

☐ E Sagittal sinus

2.17 A 34-year-old vegan presents with a six-week history of distressing paraesthesiae in the hands and legs. In the last two weeks, her gait has become unsteady and she feels her legs have become weak. On examination, vibration and joint position sense is impaired in the lower limbs. Her legs show increased tone, a mild symmetrical proximal loss of power, hyperreflexia and bilateral upgoing plantars. Her gait is ataxic. What nutritional deficiency is the likely cause of her problems?

- ☐ A Folic acid
- ☐ B Iron
- ☐ C Pyridoxine
- ☐ D Thiamine
- ☐ E Vitamin B12

2.18 A 29-year-old man presents with acute onset of wrist drop six weeks after breaking his leg. You find weakness of forearm extension, wrist and finger extension and loss of the triceps and brachioradialis reflexes, but with little sensory loss. Which one of the following branches of the brachial plexus is most likely to be affected?

- ☐ A Axillary
- ☐ B Dorsal scapular
- ☐ C Median
- ☐ D Radial
- ☐ E Ulnar

2.19 A 52-year-old man has been suffering from progressive forgetfulness and unsteadiness of gait for two months. You observe spontaneous myoclonic twitching of his fingers, and elicit startle myoclonus to a loud noise. Neuropsychological examination reveals profound impairment of memory, attention and language function. Which one of the following is the MOST likely underlying diagnosis?

- ☐ A Alzheimer's disease
- ☐ B Creutzfeldt-Jacob disease
- ☐ C Myoclonic epilepsy
- ☐ D Pick's disease
- ☐ E Subacute sclerosing panencephalitis

2.20 A 20-year-old man complains of an increasingly frequent irresistible urge to sleep several times a day, usually after a meal. After a brief nap he feels refreshed, but is increasingly disturbed that the episodes occur in embarrassing or unusual situations. He has occasionally experienced sudden weakness of the neck muscles and knees when laughing, sometimes causing him to fall to the floor. There are no neurological signs. What treatment is likely to be indicated?

- ☐ A Adrenaline
- ☐ B Bromocriptine
- ☐ C Dextroamphetamine
- ☐ D Diazepam
- ☐ E Imipramine

NEUROLOGY: MULTIPLE CHOICE QUESTIONS

Mark your answers with a tick (True) or a cross (False) in the box provided.

2.21   In Creutzfeldt-Jakob disease (CJD)

☐ A   12% of cases are familial

☐ B   increased CSF protein is often found

☐ C   periodic sharp waves on the EEG are characteristic

☐ D   cortical blindness may occur

☐ E   death usually occurs within 12 months of onset

2.22   In multiple sclerosis

☐ A   oligoclonal bands in the CSF and serum would not support the diagnosis

☐ B   low amplitude visual evoked potentials would strongly support a demyelinating optic nerve lesion

☐ C   prognosis is worse for men

☐ D   onset with sensory symptoms heralds a good prognosis

☐ E   beta-interferon decreases the relapse rate

2.23   Normal pressure hydrocephalus (NPH)

☐ A   commonly presents with papilloedema with no focal signs

☐ B   is characterised by the early onset of urinary incontinence

☐ C   characteristically presents with dementia and gait disturbance

☐ D   is demonstrable on CT scan by hydrocephalus with a normal sized fourth ventricle

☐ E   may be improved by ventricular shunting

2.24   The following are true with regard to pyramidal weakness:

☐ A   hip flexors are often weaker than knee flexors

☐ B   ankle clonus is only present when the ankle jerks are brisk

☐ C   wrist flexors will usually overcome wrist extensors

☐ D   it may occur in the absence of any sensory signs

☐ E   it is often present in syringomyelia

2.25 In motor neurone disease (MND)

- ☐ A   sensory symptoms at onset do not exclude the diagnosis
- ☐ B   peripheral sensory conduction velocities are normal
- ☐ C   the function of the glossopharyngeal nerve is frequently affected
- ☐ D   the onset of bulbar palsy indicates a poor prognosis
- ☐ E   the abdominal reflexes are usually preserved

2.26 In the spinal cord

- ☐ A   inputs from the lumbar spine nerve roots lie medial to those from the thoracic region in the spinothalamic tracts
- ☐ B   a lesion of the anterior spinal artery will cause loss of pain sensation and hyperreflexia
- ☐ C   multiple sclerosis causes demyelination of the central grey matter
- ☐ D   syringomyelia may cause the same symptoms and signs as an ependymoma
- ☐ E   the posterior spinal artery is rarely damaged

2.27 Gait ataxia

- ☐ A   is a sign of a cerebellar hemisphere lesion
- ☐ B   may be the presenting feature of benign intracranial hypertension
- ☐ C   is a presenting sign of cerebellar ectopia
- ☐ D   occurs as a feature of carbamazepine toxicity
- ☐ E   occurs in cerebellar vermis lesions

2.28 In the carpal tunnel syndrome

- ☐ A   there is increased latency of the median sensory action potential
- ☐ B   wasting of the whole of the thenar eminence occurs
- ☐ C   Tinel's sign is usually negative
- ☐ D   there is delay in the median distal motor latency
- ☐ E   in a severe case there will be weakness of extensor pollicis brevis

2.29 **Vertical nystagmus**

☐ A   if upbeating, may indicate cerebellar tonsillar ectopia

☐ B   may occur with phenytoin toxicity

☐ C   if downbeating, indicates a lesion at the foramen magnum

☐ D   when present in an unconscious patient indicates a thalamic lesion

☐ E   may present with the symptom of oscillopsia

2.30 **The following inherited disorders are known to have triplet repeats as their genetic abnormality:**

☐ A   dystrophia myotonica

☐ B   Huntington's chorea

☐ C   fragile X syndrome

☐ D   multiple system atrophy

☐ E   Gerstmann's syndrome

2.31 **Focal delta (slow) wave activity on EEG**

☐ A   is a common normal finding in adults

☐ B   indicates the presence of a focal structural lesion

☐ C   indicates the need for further investigation

☐ D   is found after a major cerebral infarction

☐ E   indicates the presence of epilepsy

2.32 **A tremor of the outstretched hands**

☐ A   is characteristic of Parkinson's disease

☐ B   responds to propranolol

☐ C   is often familial and benign

☐ D   may be worsened by anxiety

☐ E   is improved by primidone

2.33   After a major cerebral infarction

☐ A   a CT scan usually shows a low attenuation area within 2 hours

☐ B   the unenhanced scan may be normal in the second week

☐ C   contrast enhancement on the CT scan is maximal in the second week

☐ D   a mass effect from ischaemic oedema is seen on the CT scan in the first 6 hours

☐ E   carotid arteriography may be normal

2.34   After aneurysmal subarachnoid haemorrhage (SAH)

☐ A   the syndrome of inappropriate ADH secretion may occur

☐ B   the peak risk for secondary ischaemic complications is immediately after the haemorrhage

☐ C   the risk of rebleeding is maximal in the month following the stroke

☐ D   a catecholamine surge can cause direct myocardial damage

☐ E   if the patient is comatose, referral for early aneurysm clipping is generally advised

2.35   Benign intracranial hypertension (BIH)

☐ A   may present with transient visual obscurations

☐ B   is a complication of anorexia nervosa

☐ C   is associated with enlarged cerebral ventricles on CT scan

☐ D   may complicate vitamin D toxicity

☐ E   is treated by repeated lumbar puncture

2.36   The following are good prognostic indicators in head injury:

☐ A   low Glasgow coma scale 24 hours after injury

☐ B   presence of a skull fracture

☐ C   history of alcohol consumption

☐ D   absent somatosensory evoked responses

☐ E   high cerebral blood flow 48 hours post injury

2.37   Trigeminal neuralgia

- ☐ A   if associated with multiple sclerosis (MS), often has no trigger spots
- ☐ B   if associated with MS may be difficult to treat
- ☐ C   may respond to phenytoin
- ☐ D   is more common in patients with causalgia
- ☐ E   if secondary to nerve compression is usually caused by root entry zone nerve damage

2.38   Central pontine myelinolysis

- ☐ A   is confined to the pons
- ☐ B   is associated with Wernicke's encephalopathy
- ☐ C   is associated with altered consciousness
- ☐ D   is a cause of bulbar palsy
- ☐ E   may relapse spontaneously

2.39   Regarding paraneoplastic syndromes

- ☐ A   progressive cerebellar degeneration is associated with vitamin E deficiency
- ☐ B   anti-Purkinje cell antibodies are associated with ovarian carcinoma
- ☐ C   retinal degeneration is more common than optic nerve degeneration
- ☐ D   pituitary release of ADH may cause the syndrome of inappropriate ADH secretion
- ☐ E   Cushing's syndrome secondary to ectopic ACTH does not cause myopathy

2.40   In a right-sided hypoglossal nerve palsy

- ☐ A   the protruded tongue will deviate towards the left
- ☐ B   the soft palate will deviate towards the right
- ☐ C   if the neighbouring three cranial nerves are involved, the lesion is likely to be in the region of the jugular foramen
- ☐ D   taste will be impaired over the anterior two-thirds of the tongue
- ☐ E   sensation will be impaired over the right side of the soft palate

2.41   After intervertebral disc prolapse

- [ ] A   sensory loss is accompanied by reduced sensory action potentials in the relevant root distribution
- [ ] B   pain is felt in the muscles innervated by the damaged nerve root
- [ ] C   in the lumbar region an extensor plantar response may occur
- [ ] D   in the lumbar region loss of bladder function may result
- [ ] E   loss of the ankle reflex indicates an S1 root lesion

2.42   In the treatment of headache

- [ ] A   sumatriptan is an analgesic
- [ ] B   sumatriptan should only be given within two hours of a migraine attack
- [ ] C   methysergide may cause obstructive nephropathy
- [ ] D   long-acting beta blockers are often helpful in migraine
- [ ] E   ergot derivatives no longer have a role in migraine management

2.43   Myasthenia gravis

- [ ] A   is caused by autoantibodies directed against acetylcholine
- [ ] B   in older men responds to thymectomy, especially if a thymoma is present
- [ ] C   responds to high dose steroid therapy
- [ ] D   may be worsened by aminoglycoside antibiotics
- [ ] E   may be treated by long-term edrophonium therapy

2.44   In Bell's palsy

- [ ] A   the majority recover without residual weakness
- [ ] B   a complete facial weakness is a poor prognostic sign
- [ ] C   if the palsy is complete, tarsorrhaphy is usually required to protect the cornea
- [ ] D   mild sensory symptoms at onset are a common feature
- [ ] E   electrophysiological tests may be helpful prognostically

2.45   After a single unprovoked seizure in adult life

☐ A   a patient should not drive for one year

☐ B   a normal EEG excludes epilepsy

☐ C   life-long anticonvulsants are usually started

☐ D   an EEG within 24 hours will usually show signs of epilepsy

☐ E   a cerebral tumour is the most likely cause

PSYCHIATRY

'Best of Five'

M. Zoha MBChB MRCPsych
Honorary Lecturer in Psychiatry
Imperial College Higher Psychiatric Training Scheme
London

MCQs

Richard S Hopkins MRCPsych
Lecturer in Psychiatry and
Honorary Senior Registrar
Withington Hospital
Manchester

PSYCHIATRY: 'BEST OF FIVE' QUESTIONS

For each of the questions select the ONE most appropriate answer from the options provided.

3.1   **A 24-year-old man, recently admitted to a medical ward, now discloses that he is a heroin addict. He is demanding you help alleviate his withdrawal symptoms otherwise he will self-discharge. There are no contraindications to a pharmacological approach. Which one of the following would you consider the most appropriate to treat his withdrawal symptoms?**

☐ A   Bupropion

☐ B   Chlorpromazine

☐ C   Diamorphine

☐ D   Lofexidine

☐ E   Oxazepam

3.2   **A 30-year-old woman presents claiming her heart is failing. You find no abnormalities on physical examination but you elicit a number of abnormalities on mental state examination. The presence of which one of the following abnormalities lends most weight to a diagnosis of schizophrenia?**

☐ A   Catatonia

☐ B   Gustatory hallucinations

☐ C   Primary delusion

☐ D   Neologisms

☐ E   Tangential responses to questioning

3.3   **A 22-year-old woman of Indian origin is admitted as an emergency because of dehydration and very low body weight. She gives a long history of low weight, poor appetite and frequent nausea and vomiting. Which one of the following would make you most likely to suspect a diagnosis of anorexia nervosa?**

☐ A   Acknowledgement of being severely underweight

☐ B   Avoidance of Western food

☐ C   Body Mass Index (BMI) of 17

☐ D   Minimal appetite

☐ E   Self-induced vomiting

3.4 A 57-year-old married male with chronic renal failure describes poor energy levels and disturbed sleep. He goes on to describe anhedonia, guilt and hopelessness and appears unhappy. You believe he is depressed. The patient will not consider antidepressants, but agrees to talk to a therapist. Which one of the following psychological treatments is likely to be most effective?

- ☐ A Cognitive behavioural therapy
- ☐ B Family therapy
- ☐ C Psychoanalysis
- ☐ D Psychodynamic therapy
- ☐ E Supportive therapy

3.5 You are reviewing a 26-year-old woman with poorly controlled diabetes. She attends appointments erratically and you decide compliance should be optimised. In considering reasons for poor attendance, which one of the following would lead you to think agoraphobia was a possible reason?

- ☐ A Anxiety in crowded places
- ☐ B Anxiety in enclosed spaces
- ☐ C Anxiety in social situations
- ☐ D Free-floating anxiety
- ☐ E Unpredictable panic attacks

3.6 A 38-year-old colleague complains of being under considerable stress at work and fears that he is becoming mentally unwell. He describes a number of recent unusual experiences. Which one of the following would most lead you to suspect the presence of a psychotic disorder?

- ☐ A Depersonalisation
- ☐ B Derealisation
- ☐ C Hypnagogic hallucinations
- ☐ D Hypnopompic hallucinations
- ☐ E Thought alienation

3.7   A 19-year-old man admitted four days ago appears to be experiencing auditory hallucinations and thought broadcasting and has expressed persecutory delusions to the nursing staff. His girlfriend admits he has experimented with a drug of abuse prior to admission. Which one of the following drugs is most likely to produce a schizophreniform psychosis?

☐   A   Amphetamine

☐   B   Cannabis

☐   C   Heroin

☐   D   LSD

☐   E   Psilocybin

3.8   You are reviewing a 56-year-old woman with angina in clinic. She was widowed one month earlier and you are concerned about the state of her mental health. Which one of the following would make you most concerned that this lady was demonstrating pathological grief?

☐   A   Inability to feel sadness

☐   B   Intense yearning for her dead husband

☐   C   Loss of appetite

☐   D   Poor sleep

☐   E   Visions of her dead husband

3.9   A 30-year-old male political refugee has been attending hospital for several months complaining of abdominal pains. Despite extensive investigations, no organic cause has been identified. Further history taking leads you to query the relevance of possible psychological factors. Which one of the following features would most support a diagnosis of post-traumatic stress disorder (PTSD)?

☐   A   Believing his persecutors have followed him to the UK

☐   B   Diurnal variation of mood

☐   C   Early morning wakening

☐   D   Intrusive flashbacks

☐   E   Panic attacks

3.10 A 78-year-old lady recently diagnosed with dementia appears to you to be depressed. You take a history and then perform a cognitive and mental state examination. Which one of the following abnormalities is most likely to make you consider a diagnosis of depressive pseudodementia rather than dementia?

☐ A   Global memory loss

☐ B   Good effort at testing

☐ C   Poor concentration

☐ D   Poor historian

☐ E   Topographical disorientation

3.11 A 45-year-old lady has been complaining of multiple, varying gastrointestinal symptoms for three years. Despite extensive investigations and second opinions, she refuses to accept there is no physical explanation for her symptoms. She complains her life has been completely disrupted because of her symptoms and wants more tests to seek an answer. From the information given, which one of the following diagnoses is most appropriate?

☐ A   Conversion disorder

☐ B   Dissociative disorder

☐ C   Hypochondriacal disorder

☐ D   Hysterical disorder

☐ E   Somatisation disorder

3.12 Which one of the following is the most common psychiatric complication in multiple sclerosis?

☐ A   Euphoria

☐ B   Intellectual deterioration

☐ C   Major depressive episode

☐ D   Psychotic episode

☐ E   Suicide

3.13   A 26-year-old primigravida has been referred urgently by her GP. The GP's letter states she has had persistent, recurrent vomiting. Her appetite has been poor and she has eaten very little for several weeks. The GP's letter also states she has been appearing increasingly confused. Cognitive examination reveals clear consciousness, temporal disorientation, intact registration and impaired five-minute recall. With regard to the cognitive deficits, what is the most likely diagnosis?

- [ ] A   Acute organic brain syndrome
- [ ] B   Creutzfeldt-Jakob disease
- [ ] C   Frontal lobe syndrome
- [ ] D   Korsakoff's syndrome
- [ ] E   Pre-senile dementia

3.14   A mother accompanies her 30-year-old son to clinic. He has been referred for poor energy levels and fatigue. You discover he has previously been treated for schizophrenia but no longer attends psychiatric follow up. Assessment and investigations reveal no obvious cause for lethargy and you suspect the patient may be suffering negative symptoms of schizophrenia. Which one of the following is not a feature of negative schizophrenia?

- [ ] A   Alogia
- [ ] B   Anhedonia
- [ ] C   Avolition
- [ ] D   Blunting of affect
- [ ] E   Negativism

3.15   A 74-year-old man has been referred to you, as over the past few weeks his behaviour has been becoming increasingly bizarre. As part of your assessment you perform a cognitive examination. Which one of the following abnormalities is most suggestive of frontal lobe dysfunction?

- [ ] A   Hypersomnia
- [ ] B   Impaired five-minute recall
- [ ] C   Perseverating responses
- [ ] D   Right-left disorientation
- [ ] E   Sensory dysphasia

3.16 **Which one of the following conditions is least likely to concern you with regard to suicide risk?**

- [ ] A   Chronic renal failure
- [ ] B   Obsessive-compulsive disorder
- [ ] C   Opiate dependence
- [ ] D   Peptic ulcer disease
- [ ] E   Schizophrenia

3.17 **A 32-year-old man with no known history of mental illness is presenting in a highly agitated state. He appears to be experiencing distressing hallucinations and persecutory delusions. His behaviour is becoming increasingly aggressive and is no longer manageable. Which one of the following would be the most appropriate initial pharmacological intervention?**

- [ ] A   IM chlorpromazine
- [ ] B   IM diazepam
- [ ] C   IM haloperidol
- [ ] D   IM lorazepam
- [ ] E   IV haloperidol

3.18 **A 38-year-old man admitted after a fall continues to complain of memory loss one week after the injury. At the ward round, dissociative amnesia is queried as a possibility. Which one of the following features would most strongly support this diagnosis?**

- [ ] A   Fluctuating awareness
- [ ] B   Fluctuating consciousness
- [ ] C   Fluctuating recall
- [ ] D   Predominant distress
- [ ] E   Temporal disorientation

3.19 **A 33-year-old woman's behaviour on an inpatient ward is becoming increasingly unusual. She appears to be over-involved with other patients' management and reacts irritably when requested to return to her bed by staff. Nurses also report she has had very little sleep or food and that her speech makes little sense. After speaking to the patient, you agree her speech is difficult to comprehend and suspect a manic episode. Which one of the following descriptions of speech lends additional weight to the diagnosis?**

- ☐ A   Sentences include overly detailed descriptions of events
- ☐ B   Sentences spoken are connected by clanging
- ☐ C   Sentences spoken are connected obliquely
- ☐ D   There is repetition of a phrase several times
- ☐ E   There is sudden stopping of speech mid-sentence, followed by a new thought

3.20 **A 29-year-old man refuses to undress and lie on a couch for a physical examination. He states that the couch is dirty and that he does not want to risk getting an infection. Which one of the following features would most lead you to suspect a diagnosis of obsessive-compulsive disorder?**

- ☐ A   Acknowledging this belief is irrational, but still refusing
- ☐ B   Believing all hospital couches are contaminated by bacteria and are an infection risk
- ☐ C   Having a panic attack when approaching the couch
- ☐ D   Hearing a voice telling him the couch is infected
- ☐ E   Performing an elaborate, enjoyable prayer ritual before undressing

3.21 **One year after a severe head injury, which one of the following cognitive deficits is most likely to be present?**

- ☐ A   Disorder of executive functioning
- ☐ B   Fluent dysphasia
- ☐ C   Non-fluent dysphasia
- ☐ D   Non-verbal IQ loss
- ☐ E   Short-term memory loss

3.22   A patient on long-term lithium treatment for prophylaxis of bipolar
        affective disorder is complaining of feeling unwell. You wish to exclude
        lithium toxicity as a possible diagnosis. Which one of the following
        abnormalities is most likely to indicate toxicity?

☐   A   Ataxia

☐   B   Diarrhoea

☐   C   Metallic taste

☐   D   Oedema

☐   E   Tremor

3.23   A General Practitioner has finally referred a 49-year-old woman to clinic
        for long-standing weakness of her left arm. The GP confirms this symptom
        has been present for three years. Following your assessment, you suspect a
        motor conversion disorder. Which one of the following features would not
        lend weight to the diagnosis?

☐   A   A state of indifference to the paralysis

☐   B   An obvious precipitant

☐   C   Fasciculations

☐   D   Muscle wasting

☐   E   Significant secondary gain

3.24   A 24-year-old woman has been brought to hospital after collapsing. She
        appears physically well but says she has not been eating much. You suspect
        an eating disorder may have contributed to her presentation and take a
        detailed history. Which one of the following statements would not be true
        of bulimia nervosa?

☐   A   Compensatory behaviour to counteract the fattening effect of food must
        be present

☐   B   There are frequent episodes of fasting

☐   C   There are overvalued ideas of shape/weight

☐   D   There is a loss of control over eating

☐   E   The majority of cases are preceded by anorexia nervosa

3.25 **Nursing staff report that a recently admitted inpatient has been complaining of hearing voices. He has a known history of alcohol dependence syndrome. Which one of the following features would most support a diagnosis of alcoholic hallucinosis?**

☐ A Hallucinations appear as part of an alcohol withdrawal syndrome

☐ B Hallucinations are not generally distressing

☐ C Hallucinations are third person auditory

☐ D Hallucinations continue for more than six months

☐ E Hallucinations must occur in clear consciousness

PSYCHIATRY: MULTIPLE CHOICE QUESTIONS

Mark your answers with a tick (True) or a cross (False) in the box provided.

3.26   Fragile X syndrome is associated with the following features:

- A   autosomal dominant inheritance
- B   male predominance
- C   bat ears
- D   the possibility of antenatal detection
- E   hyperkinetic syndrome

3.27   In systemic lupus erythematosus (SLE)

- A   cerebral manifestations occur in less than 10% of cases
- B   schizophreniform psychosis is the commonest psychiatric manifestation
- C   psychiatric symptoms are almost always due to cerebral arteritis
- D   psychiatric symptoms usually precede fever and arthralgia
- E   cerebral involvement is an indicator of poor prognosis

3.28   The following statements about mental retardation are true:

- A   in mild retardation, subcultural influences are pre-eminent
- B   there is an increased risk of psychosis
- C   treatment for phenylketonuria should be continued for life
- D   the features of cretinism are present at birth
- E   neurofibromatosis is characteristically associated with self mutilation

3.29   In families of schizophrenic patients

- A   there is an increased rate of depression
- B   twins are more often mentally ill than non-twins
- C   adoption does not reduce the genetic risk
- D   alcoholism occurs more often than expected
- E   when the proband develops the disease late in life, the risk to relatives is reduced

3.30   The following are essential elements of the alcohol dependence syndrome:

- ☑ A   a compulsion to drink
- ☑ B   an altered tolerance to alcohol
- ☒ C   changing from beers to spirits
- ☑ D   relief drinking
- ☑ E   reinstatement after abstinence

3.31   Recognised treatments for acute mania include

- ☑ A   chlorpromazine
- ☑ B   lithium carbonate
- ☑ C   ECT – electroconvulsive therapy
- ☑ D   carbamazepine
- ☑ E   procyclidine

3.32   Features of delirium tremens (DTs) include

- ☑ A   symptoms peaking 3–4 days after abstinence from alcohol
- ☒ B   a mortality of 50%
- ☑ C   Lilliputian hallucinations
- ☑ D   hypomagnesaemia
- ☑ E   insomnia

3.33   Tardive dyskinesia

- ☑ A   is associated with previous brain damage
- ☑ B   occurs in most patients on long-term neuroleptic treatment
- ☑ C   is commoner in men
- ☑ D   is associated with reduced life expectancy in severe schizophrenia
- ☑ E   invariably improves on stopping the offending neuroleptic

3.34 **On general medical wards**

- [x] A at least one in ten patients has depression
- [x] B medical students are better than nurses at detecting psychiatric disorder
- [x] C about one in five patients have alcohol problems
- [x] D medical outcome is affected by the presence of psychiatric disorder
- [x] E most patients who have taken a drug overdose require inpatient assessment in a psychiatric unit

3.35 **Electroconvulsive treatment**

- [ ] A is known to produce long-term memory impairment in patients when compared with untreated depressives
- [x] B is not safe in patients over 80 years of age
- [ ] C is of no use in neurotic depression
- [x] D is more successful in depression when delusions are present
- [ ] E has been validated in double blind trials

3.36 **Puerperal psychosis**

- [x] A has been called 'maternity blues'
- [x] B recurs in the majority of later pregnancies
- [ ] C is significantly increased after obstetric complications
- [ ] D should be managed by separation of mother and baby in most cases
- [x] E may be accompanied by clouding of consciousness

3.37 **Characteristic features of endogenous depression include**

- [ ] A incongruity of mood and thinking
- [x] B early morning waking
- [x] C failure to respond to chlorpromazine therapy
- [x] D feelings of worthlessness
- [ ] E loss of libido

3.38   Factors which increase the risk of suicide include

☑ A   advancing age

☑ B   social class I

☑ C   the presence of hopelessness

☑ D   antisocial personality disorder

☑ E   talking about suicidal ideas

3.39   Recognised features of anorexia nervosa include

☑ A   increased plasma cortisol

☒ B   frequent structural abnormalities of the hypothalamus

☑ C   male hypersexuality

☑ D   hypokalaemia

☑ E   total loss of body hair

3.40   Panic attacks

☑ A   usually have clearly identifiable precipitants

☑ B   are important in the aetiology of social phobia

☑ C   are characterised by an impending feeling of doom

☒ D   are associated with mitral valve prolapse

☑ E   respond primarily to behavioural interventions

3.41   Clinical features of delirium often include

☑ A   decreased motor activity

☑ B   diurnal variation in symptoms

☐ C   perseveration

☒ D   a catastrophic reaction

☑ E   hallucinations

3.42   Recognized treatments for schizophrenia include

☑ A   psychodynamic psychotherapy

☑ B   clozapine

☑ C   family therapy

☑ D   Depo-Provera

☒ E   psychosurgery

3.43 **The following drugs, pharmacological actions and clinical effects are related:**

  A   amitriptyline, alpha1-adrenergic receptor antagonism, postural hypotension

  B   haloperidol, dopamine D1-receptor antagonism, antipsychotic effect

  C   tranylcypromine, irreversible blockade of monoamine oxidase, 'the cheese reaction'

  D   diazepam, GABA A agonism, anxiolytic effect

  E   lithium, inhibitor of adenylyl cyclase activation by ADH, polyuria

3.44 **Neuroleptic malignant syndrome**

  A   is characterised by hyperthermia and muscular rigidity

  B   can occur when tricyclics alone are administered

  C   most commonly occurs after haloperidol treatment

  D   is usually fatal

  E   responds to treatment with tetrabenzine

3.45 **Significant side effects of selective serotonin reuptake inhibitors (SSRIs) include**

  A   anorgasmia

  B   insomnia

  C   sweating

  D   dystonia

  E   retention of urine

3.46 **Structural imaging of the brain in schizophrenia has revealed**

  A   that degree of ventricular enlargement correlates with deficit symptoms

  B   ventricular enlargement at onset

  C   reduced volume of medial temporal lobe structures

  D   widespread grey matter volume reductions

  E   ventricular enlargement in the majority of patients when compared with unaffected siblings

3.47   The EEG in Creutzfeldt-Jacob disease (CJD)

- A   allows a confident diagnosis to be made in the early stages
- B   may show spike and wave discharges concurrent with myoclonic jerks
- C   characteristically shows synchronous triphasic sharp wave complexes and suppression of cortical background activity
- D   characteristically shows generalized low voltage fast activity or random slow activity progressing to a flat record
- E   demonstrates characteristic changes which are commonly also evident in asymptomatic first degree relatives

3.48   Insight is usually present in the following forms of abnormal illness behaviour:

- A   factitious disorder
- B   Münchausen's syndrome
- C   somatization disorder
- D   conversion disorder
- E   malingering

3.49   Huntington's chorea

- A   is caused by an X-linked gene
- B   is the commonest cause of choreiform movements first occurring in the second half of life
- C   is associated with decreased glutamic acid decarboxylase (GAD)
- D   particularly affects the cerebral cortex and basal ganglia
- E   causes rapidly progressive dementia in the majority of cases

3.50   The following features are found in the majority of cases of Down's syndrome:

- A   IQ between 20 and 50
- B   death before the age of 50 years
- C   congenital heart disease
- D   behaviour disorder
- E   flat occiput

1.1   B: Cortisol binds to the mineralocorticoid receptor

Thyroid hormone binds to two receptors, the thyroid hormone receptors alpha and beta. These are members of the nuclear receptor family, and are intracellular. Cortisol binds to both the glucocorticoid and mineralocorticoid receptors with high affinity. ACTH receptors are expressed on the adrenal and are G protein coupled. PPARgamma is essential for adipocyte differentiation, and is the target of the TZD group of Glitazone drugs. Insulin causes dimerisation of its receptors and then activates tyrosine kinase activity within the receptor.

1.2   B: Graves' disease is associated with myasthenia gravis

Toxic MNG is unlikely to respond to antithyroid drugs in the long term, and is an indication for surgery or radioiodine. Graves' disease is associated with other autoimmune diseases including myasthenia gravis. Carbimazole is not contra-indicated in pregnancy, but propylthiouracil is usually used as there are anecdotal accounts of aplasia cutis in the offspring of carbimazole treated mothers. Smoking is a risk factor for development of Graves' ophthalmopathy, and also predicts worsening of the eye disease after radioactive iodine. Radioactive iodine may exacerbate ophthalmic Graves' disease.

1.3   B: Hypoglycaemia

Adrenal insufficiency can cause hypoglycaemia, hypotension, and hypo-natraemia. It does not cause hypokalaemia. Buccal and skin pigmentation may arise due to the action of ACTH. Eosinophilia, and not neutrophilia, is found in adrenal insufficiency.

1.4   A: Amiodarone

Renal failure causes hypogonadism, and so gynaecomastia. Klinefelter's syndrome (47XXY) also causes hypogonadism. Spironolactone increases sex-hormone binding globulin, and so reduces available androgen. As a result oestrogen acts unopposed on the breast and causes gynaecomastia. Amiodarone affects the thyroid gland, and is not associated with gynaecomastia. Testicular or adrenal cancers can produce oestrogen and so cause gynaecomastia.

1.5   A: 90% of patients respond to long acting somatostatin analogue treatment

90% of patients will respond to long-acting somatostatin therapy. Microadenomas have a 90% cure rate in experienced surgical centres. Macroadenomas (>10mm diameter) have a lower cure rate of <40%. Suprasellar extension does not preclude a transsphenoidal approach, the local anatomy of the tumour is important, and is the indication (e.g. decompression of optic chiasm). Diabetes occurs in >10% of acromegalic patients. Hypercholesterolaemia is not associated with acromegaly, but cardiovascular disease and increased mortality are.

1.6   B: They are made using human B lymphocytes

Monoclonal antibodies are made by fusing a mouse B cell expressing a specific antibody with a mouse myeloma cell line. The myeloma cells give the B cells immortality, and the resulting hybridoma can be grown in vitro indefinitely. The antibodies produced can be purified and used in radioimmunoassays to measure hormones, can be used in histology to look for expression of specific proteins, and can be used therapeutically and in vitro to activate T lymphocytes.

1.7   C: They cause 'ragged red' fibres in skeletal muscle

The mitochondrial genome is small and circular. It is exclusively inherited from the mother (sperm contain no mitochondria). The genome is vulnerable to mutations, and inheritance of some mutated mitochondrial chromosomes increases the likelihood of developing disease. The tissues characteristically involved are muscle, brain, nerve and pancreatic islet. Encephalopathy, myopathy, diabetes and lactic acidosis are characteristic features.

1.8   E: It results from amplification of triplet repeats within genes

Genetic anticipation results from the amplification of unstable triplet base repeats within the coding region of genes within affected families. As a result, the size of the repeat increases with successive generations and so the age of onset of disease declines. Huntingdon's disease and fragile X syndrome are both examples. Turner's syndrome cannot be inherited, and is a chromosomal loss disease.

1.9   D: RNA polymerase II gives rise to protein encoding mRNA

Mammalian mRNA is monocistronic (i.e. each mRNA encodes one protein) in contrast to bacterial mRNA. RNA polymerase II is responsible for transcribing mRNA. Introns are transcribed, and then spliced out of the RNA to give mature mRNA before the mRNA leaves the nucleus. The genetic code is degenerate, and so multiple codons (triplets of nucleotides) encode the same amino acid. Therefore not all changes in the nucleotide sequence will give rise to changes in the protein sequence. Usually about 1% of cellular RNA is mRNA, the rest is structural.

1.10   A: Activates the NFkB transcription factor

Tumour necrosis factor (TNF) alpha can bind a p55 and a p75 receptor. The receptors are coupled to death pathways and so can induce apoptosis in susceptible cells. TNF induces activation of NFkB. TNF has been linked with insulin resistance, especially in obesity. TNF is elevated in synovial fluid, and anti TNF is useful in treating RA. TNF induces expression of other pro-inflammatory cytokines, including IL-1, and IL-6.

1.11   D: Progression from predominantly small peripheral joint disease to involve more proximal, larger joints

Rheumatoid arthritis is a multifactorial disease with an important genetic component. 20% of identical twins will develop the disease. HLA class II antigen DR4 is associated with disease, and the association is stronger with more severe disease (i.e. seropositivity; >70% of seropositive patients are DR4 +ve). The typical progression is from peripheral small joints, to later involvement of the larger joints, but sacroiliac disease is rare.

1.12   D: Patients have a characteristic reduction in circulating CD8+ T lymphocytes

PMR is a disorder of middle aged and elderly patients. Disease is rare before age 45, or after age 80. One third of patients are aged <60 years old. The onset is rapid with full development in a month. Systemic features include weight loss, night sweats, fever, fatigue and malaise and are common. Muscle enzymes and EMG are normal in PMR. Patients respond rapidly to prednisolone, but so do patients with sepsis, osteoarthritis, and rheumatoid arthritis, and so the improvement is not helpful for diagnosis. There is a characteristic loss of CD8+ T cytotoxic/suppressor cells which can persist up to a year after clinical remission.

1.13   E: Over-represented in Whipple's disease

HLA B27 is a class I HLA, or major histocompatibility antigen (MHC), and is expressed on most cells types. It is over-represented in ankylosing spondylitis (90% of patients compared to 8% of normals), Whipple's disease, reactive arthritis, psoriatic arthritis, Reiter's syndrome, and uveitis. It is not over-represented in Crohn's disease, ulcerative colitis, or Behçet's disease. Class II HLA antigens are expressed on antigen presenting cells like dendritic cells, and B lymphocytes.

1.14   C: Polyarteritis nodosa mainly affects small vessels

PAN typically affects medium sized arteries with frequent aneurysm formation. Antibodies to proteinase 3 (also known as cANCA) are exceptionally rare in non vasculitic disease. Wegener's granulomatosis affects the upper and lower airways, and the small vessels of the kidney. Churg-Strauss syndrome patients typically present with asthma and eosinophilia. An environmental agent is suggested by the seasonal change in incidence shown in North America.

1.15   D: High frequencies of disease are seen in women of Chinese ancestry

SLE is commoner in women with African, Chinese, Asian or South American Indian ancestry, compared to North Europeans. Women are affected more frequently than men (9:1), and there is an increased incidence in Klinefelter's syndrome (47XXY). The skin is a target organ in 70% of cases. 15% of the normal population have Raynaud's phenomenon, in SLE the incidence is between 20 and 30%. C reactive protein is not raised in SLE.

1.16   C: Hyaline casts consist of Tamm-Horsfall protein

Hyaline casts are made of Tamm-Horsfall protein, a mucoprotein secreted by the distal convoluted tubule. They are found in normal urine, more so after exercise, during febrile illness, and after loop diuretics. Oxalate crystals are found in normal urine if it is allowed to stand. When present in freshly passed urine, or in large amounts they indicate a predisposition to stone formation. Cystine crystals indicate cystinuria. >10 white cells per ml urine is abnormal, usually indicating urinary tract infection. A few red cells are found in normal urine, >2000 per ml is probably abnormal.

1.17   A: Acyclovir

The clearance of a drug depends on size and protein binding. Most antibiotics are small and so are dialysed, with the exception of vancomycin, amphotericin, and erythromycin. Protein bound drugs like warfarin and propranolol are not cleared.

1.18   D: Urine sodium >20 mmol/l

Pre-renal failure is caused by poor renal perfusion. The kidney retains sodium (hence urine sodium concentrations are low), and excretes urea (hence urine urea concentrations are high compared to plasma). The urine osmolality is high. Associated features of hypovolaemia should be sought, and these include postural hypotension, and decreased pulmonary wedge pressures.

1.19   B: Abdominal pain is a common presenting feature

The inheritance is autosomal dominant. Abdominal pain, spontaneous haematuria, an increase in girth, hypertension, urinary tract infection, renal colic, and renal impairment may all be the presenting features of this disease. There is no specific treatment for the condition, which will require renal replacement therapy between ages 30 and 50 in most cases. One-third of patients will have a hepatic cyst, and a few pancreatic or splenic cysts. Berry aneurysms in the cerebral circulation may cause haemorrhage in approximately 10% of patients.

1.20   E: The proximal nephron actively secretes hydrogen ions, in contrast to the distal nephron

Under normal circumstances both the proximal and distal tubule actively secrete hydrogen ions into the tubular fluid. These combine with filtered bicarbonate ions to form carbonic acid, which dissociates into water, and carbon dioxide. The carbon dioxide is reabsorbed, and used to generate bicarbonate ions, which are returned to the circulation. Approximately 90% of the filtered bicarbonate ions filtered by the glomerulus are recovered in this manner. In distal renal tubular acidosis there is a mild chronic hyperchloraemic metabolic acidosis (normal anion gap), with exacerbations of acidosis. There is failure of the distal tubule to secrete hydrogen ions, and so the urine pH seldom falls below 5.5. About 70% of patients will have nephrocalcinosis or renal calculi, distinguishing the disorder from the other renal tubular acidoses. Proximal tubular acidosis is rare as an isolated defect, and is often found with aminoaciduria, glycosuria, hyperphosphaturia and uricosuria. The condition is usually part of a Fanconi syndrome but may result from poisoning (e.g. outdated tetracycline).

1.21   D: It is a lentivirus

HIV is a lentivirus (a virus with slow progression). There are two forms, 1 and 2. Both forms cause AIDS, but disease progression is slower with type 2. The two viruses appear to have distinct evolutionary origins. The HIV viruses are retroviruses, with RNA containing genomes. HIV gains entry to the cell via a chemokine receptor, and results in depletion of CD4 cells. An adverse indicator is elevation of CD8 cells.

1.22   B: Pneumococcal otitis media is usually associated with neutrophil leukocytosis

Pneumococcus is a Gram-positive organism. Pneumococcal pneumonia has a peak in winter, probably due to low humidity, low temperature, and respiratory virus infection. Otitis media due to *Pneumococcus* is usually associated with neutrophilia, which can be helpful in diagnosis. Pneumococcal meningitis is accompanied by a high mortality rate, even with modern treatment. The disease carries at least five times greater mortality compared to meningococcal meningitis. Sickle cell disease results in hyposplenism, and so predisposes to pneumococcal disease, which can be prevented by antibody prophylaxis.

1.23   D: Meningitis is a relatively benign condition in adults

Herpes simplex consists of two types: 1 which mainly causes orofacial disease; and 2 which mainly causes genital disease. Herpes meningitis is benign, with normal adults recovering in about a week; no specific treatment is needed. Erythema multiforme frequently results from previous herpes infection. Antibody titres are only useful in retrospective diagnosis on the basis of a rising titre in the convalescent phase. The herpes viruses are double stranded DNA viruses.

1.24   B: Identification of Gram-positive diplococci on lumbar puncture suggests meningococcal meningitis

Meningococci are Gram-negative diplococci. Acute septicaemia is associated with neutrophilia, as is meningitis, leucopenia is rarely found in fulminating cases. The classic early skin lesion is a petechial rash, but as the condition deteriorates more extensive haemorrhagic lesions develop. Rifampicin eradicates nasal carriage of meningococci in 25% at 6 days, and 19% at 2 weeks. Transmission is usually by respiratory droplet, though sexual transmission is also reported.

1.25   D: Haematuria

Typhoid should be suspected in travellers with unexplained fever. The temperature shows gradual onset and reaches 39–40°C, with characteristically little diurnal variation. The most common associated feature is headache. Classically there is constipation, although most patients will experience loose stools at some time also. Features of significant infection such as myalgia, lassitude, and arthralgia are not specific. Notable features of untreated infection include altered mental state, which gives typhoid its name. Typically this includes mental apathy and can progress to agitated delirium. Nephrotyphoid is rare and so haematuria usually suggests another cause for the fever.

1.26   A: Aortic dissection is a recognised complication

Mutations in Marfan's syndrome are scattered throughout the gene on chromosome 15 that encodes fibrillin, a component of microfibrils in the extracellular matrix. The mutations are most often missense, that is, they result in an amino acid substitution. The gene contains 65 exons. Marfan's syndrome is inherited in an autosomal dominant fashion with variable expression but generally full penetrance. New mutations occur in about 15–30% of cases. Slit lamp examination is required for detection of slight lens dislocation.

1.27   E: Velocardiofacial syndrome

Aneurysms of the aorta are seen in Marfan's syndrome while intracranial Berry aneurysms are observed in polycystic kidney disease. Large vessel rupture is a recognised complication of pseudoxanthoma elasticum (usually autosomal recessive) and of type IV Ehlers-Danlos syndrome autosomal dominant). Type IV (i.e. vascular) Ehlers-Danlos syndrome results from a type 3 collagen defect, whereas the classical forms of Ehlers-Danlos syndrome result from a type 5 collagen abnormality. Pulmonary arteriovenous shunts, and their potential for spontaneous rupture, are a known complication of hereditary haemorrhagic telangiectasia.

1.28   E: There is no increase in the incidence of homosexuality

The incidence is approximately 1 in 1000 new-born males. There is no association with severe learning difficulties, though the range of IQs in affected individuals is shifted down slightly, relative to that of unaffected individuals. Verbal scores are affected most. There is no increase in the incidence of homosexuality. Breast development is present in around 25–30%. Testosterone therapy is believed to help prevent osteoporosis, in addition to increasing libido and physical activity. Testes are generally much smaller than normal and Leydig cell function is reduced. Spermatogenesis is very poor but in some cases fertilisation may be achieved by sperm aspiration or biopsy, followed by intra-cytoplasmic sperm injection (ICSI).

1.29   C: HNPCC *hMLH1*

FGFR3 (fibroblast growth factor receptor 3) is associated with achondroplasia. SMN (survival motor neurone) is the gene responsible for spinal muscular atrophy (SMA). Limb-girdle muscular dystrophy is associated with the sarcoglycans and calpain genes, while congenital muscular dystrophy is associated with the merosin gene. Hereditary non-polyposis colon cancer (HNPCC) is usually associated with mutations in either the hMLH1 or the hMSH2 gene.

1.30   D: It exists predominantly as a nucleoprotein complex

Only about 3% of nuclear DNA is coding. The coding sequences are interrupted by introns, which are removed during splicing. Hydrogen bonds mediate base-pairing, while the sugar-phosphate 'backbone' of each DNA strand is held together by covalent bonds. DNA in the nucleus is tightly wrapped around proteins called histones, thus forming a nucleoprotein complex.

BASIC SCIENCES: MULTIPLE CHOICE ANSWERS

1.31   B E

Isovolumetric contraction occurs after mitral valve closure (1st heart sound) and before aortic valve opening. Left ventricular pressure increases from 8 mmHg to 130 mmHg but in the aorta elastic recoil maintains pressure during diastole so that aortic pressure is approximately 130/75 (mean 100 mmHg). The venous C wave is due to bulging of the tricuspid valve during ventricular contraction. Ventricular filling is most rapid immediately after the A-V valves open but is augmented by atrial systole. During inspiration the ventricular ejection period is prolonged due to increased stroke volume secondary to increased venous return.

1.32   B D

3-hydroxy-3-methyl glutaryl-CoA (HMGCoA) reductase inhibitors inhibit cholesterol biosynthesis and can decrease serum LDL by 30–40%. Serum triglycerides are also reduced but to a much lesser extent and HDL is increased. Myositis can occur in up to 0.5% of patients. Fibric acid derivatives, but not statins, tend to produce improvement in glucose tolerance (especially bezafibrate) and fenofibrate reduces urate levels by a direct renal uricosuric action.

1.33   D

Losartan is an angiotensin II receptor blocker. It leads to an increase in angiotensin II. It specifically blocks the renin–angiotensin system and unlike ACE inhibitors does not increase bradykinin which has been implicated in both ACE I induced cough and angioneurotic oedema. It does however share with ACE I the side effects related to renin–angiotensin system blockade including risk of acute renal failure in renal artery stenosis and hyperkalaemia.

1.34   A B

Cystic fibrosis is an autosomal recessive disease caused by mutations to the cystic fibrosis transmembrane conductance regulator (CFTR) genes on chromosome 7. Both genes must be affected for cystic fibrosis to develop. Over 500 CFTR mutations associated with cystic fibrosis are known. Genotyping can therefore be difficult to interpret – failure to find two abnormal genes does not rule out the disease. In about 1% of those with the disease no abnormal gene can be found and in about 18% more only one abnormal gene will be identified. Even if both genes are abnormal, the individual may not have the disease because some mutations ameliorate or neutralise the primary mutation. There is a close correlation between phenotype (clinical manifestations) and the percentage of normal CFTR function: <1% severe disease and pancreatic failure; <5% pulmonary disease; <10% congenital absence of the vas deferens; >10% no abnormality.

1.35   A C D

The P50 of haemoglobin is the partial pressure of oxygen at which half the haemoglobin is oxygenated. Factors that increase the P50 will shift the haemoglobin–oxygen curve to the right releasing more O_2 to the tissues, i.e. an increased P50 reflects reduced oxygen affinity. The effect of acidosis on the oxygen affinity of haemoglobin is known as the Bohr effect. Temperature and 2,3 DPG also directly increase P50. Carbon dioxide has a minor effect on oxygen affinity – also shifting the curve to the right. Chloride ions do not have a direct effect on oxygen affinity but do increase in acidosis (the chloride shift) because of the free diffusion of HCO_3 ions out of erythrocytes.

1.36   A B C

Allergic bronchopulmonary aspergillosis typically occurs in chronic asthmatics. Inhaled *Aspergillus fumigatus* spores germinate and grow in bronchi triggering antibody production and eosinophilia. Identification of fungal hyphae in casts is diagnostic, but skin tests are also positive in 90% of cases. Bronchopulmonary aspergillosis is not a form of extrinsic allergic alveolitis, although *Aspergillus clavatus* can cause allergic alveolitis in malt workers.

1.37   None correct

Factor V Leiden results from a single amino acid substitution at position 506 of glutamine for arginine. The resultant factor V in its activated form is resistant to cleavage by the natural anticoagulant protein C. Venous thromboembolism develops in up to 40% of heterozygotes and heterozygotes account for about 15% of all thromboembolic episodes. The condition is hereditary. Unlike the antiphospholipid antibodies syndrome it is not associated with recurrent abortion.

1.38   A E

Vitamin B12 in animal food binds to a glycoprotein – intrinsic factor – which is secreted by parietal cells in the stomach and is absorbed via a specific receptor on the surface of the mucosa of the ileum. Vitamin B12 enters the ileal cells and intrinsic factor remains in the lumen. Vitamin B12, like folate, is a key enzyme in the synthesis of DNA – deficiency of either reduces the availability of methylene tetrahydrofolate polyglutamate. Lead poisoning interferes with haem and globin synthesis resulting in abnormal erythrocytes with basophilic stippling.   In pernicious anaemia there is atrophy of the gastric mucosa, achlorhydria and increased risk of both gastric carcinoids and gastric carcinoma.

1.39   B C D

Glucose-6-phosphate dehydrogenase (G6PD) is a vital enzyme in the hexose monophosphate pathway that provides glutathione in a reduced state for the red cell. Glutathione reduces oxidative stress on the red cell, maintaining membrane flexibility and avoiding oxidation of haemoglobin that would result in methaemoglobin formation. G6PD deficiency is sex linked. Deficiency of the enzyme provides protection against *Plasmodium falciparum*. Attacks of acute haemolysis are usually precipitated by drugs or infection. Haemoglobin electrophoresis is normal as is osmotic fragility.

1.40   A B D

Erythropoietin is used for the treatment of anaemia in renal failure after non-renal causes of anaemia (e.g. bone marrow infiltration, gastrointestinal blood loss and folate/B12 deficiency) have been excluded. Any alternative cause of anaemia such as iron deficiency can lead to resistance to erythropoietin and the need for higher doses of erythropoietin to achieve satisfactory haemoglobin responses. Acute infection and chronic infections (e.g. TB or osteomyelitis) are also associated with poor response to erythropoietin by mechanisms related to increased inflammatory cytokines. Hyperparathyroidism also impairs the bone marrow response to erythropoietin. Antibodies to erythropoietin have not been detected. ACE inhibitors do not affect the response to erythropoetin.

1.41   A C D

The elimination of many drugs is dependent on renal excretion. Tobramycin, acyclovir and allopurinol all accumulate to toxic levels if given at standard dose for normal renal function. Aminoglycosides result in ototoxicity and renal toxicity, acyclovir can cause a toxic encephalopathy that can lead to diagnostic confusion with herpes encephalitis and allopurinol and its metabolite oxypurinol increase the risk of a serious desquamative skin eruption in renal failure. Simvastatin and nifedipine must be used with caution in hepatic impairment.

1.42   A B D

Renal dose dopamine augments renal blood flow, glomerular filtration and natriuresis in healthy humans. It does not, however, improve renal function or outcome in acute renal failure and has not been demonstrated to protect high risk patients. Its use in these situations is therefore controversial. Renal dose dopamine can precipitate serious cardiovascular and metabolic complications in critically ill patients, including bowel ischaemia.

1.43.   A D E

Rifampicin reduces the effect of sulphonylureas by accelerating metabolism via enzyme induction. Bendrofluazide, and other thiazide and loop diuretics, cause insulin resistance and glucose intolerance. Alcohol, sulphonamide antibiotics, trimethoprim, miconazole, fibrates and sulphinpyrazone enhance the effect of sulphonylureas.

1.44   C D E

H_2 blockade does not interfere with prolactin secretion but cimetidine (not ranitidine) is a cause of gynaecomastia. In normal physiological circumstances prolactin is under tonic inhibitory control by the dopaminergic system of the hypothalamus. Dopamine depleting agents (e.g. methyldopa) and dopamine receptor blockers (e.g. metoclopramide and haloperidol) result in increased prolactin release. Oestrogens which increase the number and activity of prolactin secreting cells do not act through dopamine related mechanisms. Hypothyroidism, via thyroid stimulating hormone, frequently causes increased prolactin which is suppressed by thyroxine.

1.45   A

Adrenal insufficiency can be due to many causes including tuberculosis, autoimmune adrenalitis, systemic fungal infection, metastatic carcinoma, HIV infection, antiphospholipid syndrome, amyloidosis and acute haemorrhage in sepsis such as meningococcaemia. Rifampicin is an enzyme inducer and can unmask adrenal insufficiency. Treatment is with the smallest dose of hydrocortisone or cortisone necessary to relieve the patient's symptoms in order to avoid the side effects of glucocorticoids. Fludrocortisone is necessary in a single daily dose of 50–200 μg depending on blood pressure, serum potassium and serum renin. Adrenal autoantibodies can be detected in 70% of patients with autoimmune adrenalitis but not the other causes. Adrenomyeloneuropathy is an X-linked recessive disorder of long chain fatty acid metabolism that is characterised by spastic paraparesis and adrenal failure in young men.

1.46   B D E

Hereditary angioedema is an autosomal dominant trait characterised by low (less than 25% of normal) to undetectable functional activity of C1 inhibitor. This deficiency of C1 inhibitor permits C1s to continuously cleave its substrates, C4 and C2, producing a secondary deficiency in these proteins. Clinically the illness is characterised by recurrent episodes of subcutaneous oedema, upper respiratory tract oedema/obstruction or abdominal pain due to bowel wall oedema. Treatment of an acute attack includes fresh plasma to restore C1 inhibitor levels and support therapy. Danazol is effective in reducing episodes of angioedema.

1.47   B D

Type IV hypersensitivity (delayed hypersensitivity) reactions are initiated by T cells not antibody. Histologically, delayed–type hypersensitivity reactions consist of infiltrating lymphocytes, macrophages and occasionally eosinophils. Mast cells are not involved in Type IV hypersensitivity but are pivotal in Type I sensitivity which results in mast cell degranulation. Chronic lesions can show granulomatous reactions as in tuberculosis. Contact dermatitis is a Type IV hypersensitivity reaction. Myasthenia gravis is an antibody mediated autoimmune disease of the neuromuscular junction (Type II hypersensitivity). Type III hypersensitivity is due to immune complex formation, as in serum sickness.

1.48   A D

Rheumatoid factors (RFs) are autoantibodies against the IgG Fc, not Fab, fragment. RFs are found in both the healthy population and several disease conditions including of course rheumatoid arthritis (50–90%) and SLE (15–35%). RFs of the IsM isotype are predominant in serum and have also been found in the synovial fluid of inflamed joints in rheumatoid arthritis. RFs are distinct from antinuclear antibodies and are not acute phase proteins although following infections and immunisations, RFs can be transiently produced in healthy subjects.

1.49   B D

Internuclear ophthalmoplegia is a common brain stem lesion often resulting from demyelination. The lesion is in the medial longitudinal fasciculus and results in impaired adduction on the side of the lesion and nystagmus on abduction of the contralateral eye. It does not affect vertical gaze or the pupil.

1.50   A B E

Multiple sclerosis (MS) is an acquired defect of oligodendrocytes that are responsible for producing myelin. As a result of demyelination the normal saltatory conduction between nodes of Ranvier is impaired. In MS breakdown of the blood–brain barrier precedes both symptoms and MRI signs of demyelination. Perivascular helper T cells are found in acute MS lesions and there is abnormal MHC class II expression on macrophages and astrocytes resulting in antigen presentation and immune injury.

1.51   B C

Anti-acetylcholine receptor antibodies have a high sensitivity and specificity for myasthenia gravis. They are mainly IgG and can cross the feto-placental barrier. Their main pathogenic role is via complement dependent lysis of the post-synaptic membrane. Anti-acetylcholine receptor antibodies are of high affinity, idiotypically heterogenous and variable in antigenic specificity. They do not arise as a paraneoplastic phenomenon and do not occur in the Eaton–Lambert syndrome. Penicillamine can result in the development of antiacetylcholine receptor antibodies with or without development of myasthenia gravis.

1.52   B

Live vaccines should not be given to individuals with impaired immune response, whether caused by disease or as a result of radiotherapy, corticosteroids, or other immunosuppressive drugs. Diphtheria, hepatitis B, tetanus and pneumococcal vaccine are all inactive vaccines and are safe in immunosuppressed patients. Immunogenicity of vaccines, however, may be reduced in the immunosuppressed patient – this particularly applies to hepatitis B. Polyvalent pneumococcal polysaccharide vaccine is recommended for the immunisation of all immuno-suppressed patients. Bacillus Calmette–Guerin vaccine is a live attenuated vaccine that can cause serious mycobacterial disease in the immunocompromised. Other live vaccines include yellow fever, measles, mumps, rubella and (Sabin) polio.

1.53   A B

Schistosomiasis is endemic in many areas of the Middle East, Africa, South America and Asia. The risk of infection is directly related to exposure to fresh water containing the intermediate snail hosts. Acute infection often produces an urticarial rash and is associated with eosinophilia. The adult schistosomes usually have a life span of 3 to 5 years and do not multiply in the human host. Pathology is caused by the immunological reaction to the deposited ova which causes an intense fibrotic reaction. Treatment with praziquantel at 40 mg/kg in a single oral dose is safe and effective.

1.54 A C E

Borrelia burgdorferi is a Gram-negative microaerophilic spirochaete that requires various vertebrate and arthropod hosts for survival. It is the causative organism of Lyme disease which usually begins with flu-like or meningitis-like symptoms accompanied by a characteristic rash, erythema migrans, at the site of the tick bite. After days to weeks, the spirochaete often disseminates from the skin and can affect multiple organ systems, most commonly the joints, nervous system and heart. *B. burgdorferi* is sensitive to penicillins and treatment of choice is amoxycillin or doxycycline. Babesiosis is a tick borne protozoan disease characterised by an acute febrile illness with haemolytic anaemia as a result of multiplication of the organisms in RBCs.

1.55 D E

Alpha interferon treatment is indicated in patients with chronic hepatitis secondary to hepatitis B if there is persistent elevation of serum transaminases, detection of HBs Ag, Hbe Ag and HBV DNA in serum, chronic hepatitis in liver biopsy and compensated liver disease. A course of 4–6 months' treatment induces remission in 25% to 40% of patients. Patients with normal transaminase levels rarely respond to treatment. Transient increases in serum transaminase levels are common during therapy, especially in those in whom HBe Ag disappears. Other side effects include increased risks of bacterial infections, influenza-like reactions, chronic fatigue syndrome, autoimmune diseases and severe depression. Hepatitis D is responsive to alpha interferon but is more resistant than HBV and therefore higher doses are required.

1.56 B E

Hepatitis C is an RNA virus. The rate of chronic viral hepatitis in patients with acute hepatitis C is in the region of 80–100%. Hepatitis C is the most common cause of chronic viral hepatitis in the western world. Severe hepatitis can be present despite normal serum transaminase levels. The benefit of alpha interferon was demonstrated in non A non B hepatitis even before the discovery of HCV. Patients with HCV can develop vasculitis, cryoglobulinaemia and mesangiocapillary glomerulonephritis.

1.57   A D

Intestinal fat absorption is dependent on bile salt acids. These are detergents that emulsify coarse dietary fat globules leaving the stomach. Following this, pancreatic lipases break down the droplets leading to the formation of much smaller mixed micelles. Fatty acids, monoglycerides, phospholipids and cholesterol enter the enterocytes from the mixed micelles in the jejunum. Bile salt acids are reabsorbed in the terminal ileum. Neomycin owes its hypocholesterolaemic action to disruption of mixed micelles. The LDL receptor is not required for cholesterol absorption.

1.58   B C D E

The complement system amplifies the action of antibodies which activate complement component 1 – the classical pathway – but microbial polysaccharides can also directly activate component 3 – the alternative pathway. The consequence of activation is the assembly of the late complement components into the membrane attack complex that punches holes in the cell membrane. Complement activation has been implicated in tissue injury in a wide variety of circumstances including inflammation and ischaemia. In the normal situation, injury to human cells is reduced by inactivation of the terminal components by membrane bound complement control proteins. These control proteins are defective in paroxysmal nocturnal haemoglobinuria.

1.59   B E

Mitochondrial DNA is a double stranded, circular molecule that mutates over ten times more frequently than nuclear DNA. Each mitochondrion contains 2–10 DNA molecules. It has no introns nor an effective repair system and therefore a random mutation will usually strike a coding DNA sequence. Mitochondrial DNA is maternally inherited. Classic mitochondrial DNA diseases include Leber's optic atrophy, chronic progressive external ophthalmoplegia and mitochondrial myopathy. Systemic features of mitochondrial DNA mutations include diabetes mellitus, cardiomyopathy, lactic acidosis, Fanconi's syndrome and Wolff–Parkinson–White syndrome.

1.60   A C D

The polymerase chain reaction amplifies DNA that has first been separated into single strands by heat. Two oligonucleotide primers are then used to bind to either side of the specific areas of interest of the DNA and a polymerase enzyme catalyses the synthesis of a copy of the nucleotide sequence between the primers. The process can be repeated many times to make multiple copies of the specific gene of interest. The technique can be used to detect differences in genes – polymorphisms, presence of foreign genetic material and even RNA from either messenger RNA or RNA viruses using reverse transcriptase. The technique is highly specific for the oligonucleotide sequence used in the primers and is also of high sensitivity – contamination with only a single DNA copy can lead to false-positive results unless rigorous controls are used.

NEUROLOGY: 'BEST OF FIVE' ANSWERS

2.1   C: Multiple system atrophy

All of these diagnoses can be associated with extrapyramidal signs. Typically the triad of rigidity, resting tremor and bradykinesia is associated with Parkinson's disease. Here, the presence of additional autonomic symptoms and signs suggests a 'Parkinson's Plus' syndrome. Postural hypotension may occur in patients with Parkinson's disease, but is typically mild and secondary to (levodopa) medication. Multiple system atrophy represents a group of disorders combining Parkinsonism with moderate to severe autonomic neuropathy. In this group of disorders, the Parkinsonism is typically poorly responsive to treatment.

2.2   C: Right abducens nerve

Three cranial nerves control the upper eyelid, eye movements and pupils, the oculomotor (III), trochlear (IV) and abducens (VI). Horizontal diplopia implies a weakness of the horizontally acting muscles, vertical diplopia the vertical acting muscles. Diplopia is maximal in the direction of action of the weak muscle, and when the eye to which the weak muscle belongs is covered then the outer (false) image is obscured. Thus in this case, the diplopia is caused by a weak right lateral rectus, thus indicating right abducens palsy. This is most likely caused by poorly controlled diabetes mellitus.

2.3   E: Temporal lobe uncus across the tentorium

Space occupying lesions can impair consciousness either through direct extension of the lesion into the midbrain and brainstem, or more commonly by lateral and downward displacement of these structures with or without herniation of the medial part of the temporal lobe through the tentorium. This lateral displacement typically crushes the upper midbrain against the opposite free edge of the tentorium, causing an upgoing plantar ipsilateral to the hemispheric lesions. All forms of brainstem herniation can cause depression of respiration, extensor posturing and bilateral upgoing plantars. The uncal syndrome differs mainly in that early drowsiness is accompanied or preceded by unilateral papillary dilatation, often (but not always) due to compression of the oculomotor nerve by the herniated uncus.

2.4   C: Posterior inferior cerebellar artery

Ipsilateral Horner's syndrome and contralateral loss of pain and temperature sensation indicate damage in the dorsolateral region of the medulla, known as Wallenberg's syndrome. Lower vestibular nuclei are often involved, resulting in vertigo, vomiting and nystagmus; involvement of the inferior cerebellar peduncle will result in ipsilateral limb ataxia. This medullary syndrome is most often caused by occlusion of the posterior inferior cerebellar artery, although in some cases an occlusion of the parent vertebral artery can be responsible.

2.5   A: Acoustic neuroma

A cerebellopontine angle lesion is indicated by the combination of absent corneal reflex and sensorineural deafness. No other single central lesion could account for these signs. Lesions arising in the pons such as multiple sclerosis or brainstem astrocytoma are likely to present with more complex neurological signs. Similarly, extrinsic lesions such as basilar artery aneurysm or nasopharyngeal carcinoma are more likely to present with isolated single compressive cranial nerve lesions.

2.6   C: Left thalamic metastasis

The dense sensory impairment described here is typical for a space occupying thalamic lesion and the progressive history over several months makes metastasis more likely than either demyelination or stroke. Sensory loss caused by a cortical lesion is rarely complete.

2.7   A: Craniopharyngioma

Craniopharyngiomas compress the optic chiasm from above and behind, producing a bitemporal hemianopia that spreads up from the lower fields into the upper fields. In adults, pituitary dysfunction secondary to craniopharyngioma is variable, but it may block the third ventricle causing hydrocephalus and dementia. Pituitary macroadenomas cause a bitemporal hemianopia typically spreading down from the upper fields as the optic chiasm is damaged from below.

2.8   A: Common peroneal nerve

The common peroneal nerve is most often damaged by compression at the fibula neck, where it winds around the bone. The nerve is motor to tibialis anterior and the peronei, causing weakness of dorsiflexion and eversion respectively. As nerve roots L5 and S1 control these movements differentiation from an L5 root lesion requires demonstration of intact eversion in the presence of severe weakness of dorsiflexion. The common peroneal is sensory to a small patch of skin on the dorsum of the foot between big and second toes, but often there is little or no sensory loss detectable clinically.

2.9   C: Meningococcal meningitis

This patient has an acute bacterial meningitis, and is predisposed to infection due to his splenectomy. Meningococcal meningitis is the most likely diagnosis, due to the characteristic petechiae and purpura. Although these skin manifestations can also be seen occasionally with haemophilus and pneumococcal meningitis, they are much more common in meningococcal meningitis.

2.10   D: Episodic memory deficit

The gradual development of forgetfulness is the major symptom of Alzheimer's disease, and is characterized on neuropsychological testing by a deficit of episodic memory. Other failures of cortical function, including all the disorders here, may be manifest but typically occur later in the course of the disease. Visual hallucinations are often a prominent feature of a less common form of dementia, corticobasal degeneration; and frontal syndromes such as disinhibition, together with progressive language impairment, are seen in Pick's disease.

2.11   A: Huntington's chorea

Progressive chorea, emotional disturbance and dementia with onset in the fourth decade are typical of Huntington's chorea. Patients may lack or conceal a family history; diagnosis is usually easy, as the mutation (CAG repeat expansion in the Huntington gene) has been identified. The other diagnoses listed here can cause an extrapyramidal movement disorder, but choreiform movements are less common and/or prominent, and intellectual decline is not typically a presenting feature.

2.12   C: Left parietal lobe

This woman has a partial Gerstmann syndrome, affecting the dominant (left) parietal lesion. The characteristic features are inability to name the fingers of the two hands (finger agnosia), confusion of left and right sides of the body, inability to calculate (dyscalculia) or write (dysgraphia). Damage to the superior part of the optic radiation in the underlying white matter causes a contralateral homonymous lower quadrantanopia (c.f. homonymous superior quadrantanopia following temporal lesions). Often the patient will be unaware of the visual field deficit.

2.13   D: Haeme

Severe, symmetric polyneuropathy together with abdominal pain and neuro-psychiatric symptoms (or confusion) is typical of acute intermittent porphyria. This is a disorder of haeme metabolism inherited as an autosomal dominant syndrome, with attacks often precipitated by drugs such as oestrogens, phenytoin and sulphonamides. The neuropathy often involves the motor nerves more severely than the sensory; symptoms may begin in the arms or legs, usually distally but occasionally also in the proximal limb girdle.

2.14   B: Guillain-Barré syndrome

Guillain-Barré syndrome (GBS) is an acute ascending polyneuropathy; as here, typically sensory symptoms are out of proportion to the weakness. Areflexia is characteristic and progression can be rapid with respiratory failure and death. The most immediate diagnostic problem is to differentiate GBS from acute spinal cord compression (which would produce an upper motor neurone lesion in the legs with hyperreflexia and upgoing plantars, and does not produce facial weakness). CSF is typically acellular or with a mild lymphocytosis, but with a grossly elevated protein.

2.15   A: Carbamazepine

This woman has complex partial seizures, with a typical aura followed by loss of consciousness and subsequent post-ictal confusion. While unconscious during the fit, her behaviour shows automatisms and semi-purposive features. Carbamazepine is the drug of choice for complex partial seizures, or sometimes sodium valproate. Phenytoin can be successful but can also sometimes worsen complex partial seizures. Lamotrigine, vigabatrin and gabapentin are also useful, but only as second-line agents.

2.16   E: Sagittal sinus

Parasagittal biparietal or bifrontal hemorrhagic infarctions are common sequelae of sagittal sinus thrombosis. Oral contraceptives, the immediate postpartum period, hypercoagulable states and dehydration all predispose to sagittal sinus thrombosis. The presence of multiple lesions not in typical arterial territories, and the prominent epileptic fits, favour this diagnosis.

2.17   E: Vitamin B12

Subacute combined degeneration of the spinal cord, due to vitamin B12 deficiency, results in degeneration of the posterior columns (vibration and joint position sense) followed by progressive development of upper motor neurone signs in the legs. Spinal cord involvement is roughly symmetrical, but can progress to dementia and visual impairment due to optic neuropathy. Thiamine deficiency may give rise to Wernicke's syndrome (ophthalmoplegia, ataxia and confusion), or to beri-beri (peripheral neuropathy). Pyridoxine deficiency gives rise to a chronic painful sensorimotor neuropathy. This can be caused by administration of isoniazid (for tuberculosis) which increases the excretion of pyridoxine; hence isoniazid is always administered in conjunction with pyridoxine.

2.18   D: Radial

The radial nerve in the axilla is often damaged by the incorrect use of a crutch, which causes weakness of all the radial nerve innervated muscles. In addition to triceps and the wrist and finger extensors, there is also weakness of brachioradialis. Triceps is only variably involved, for reasons that are unclear.

2.19   B: Creutzfeldt-Jacob disease

This is a rapidly progressive and severe dementia associated with cerebellar ataxia, diffuse myoclonic jerks, and other neurological abnormalities. Myoclonus is typical and progressive, even during the later stages when the patient is stuporose or comatose. The disease is invariably fatal, usually within a few months. The EEG pattern is characteristic but diagnosis relies on either specialised tests for prion protein in CSF, or direct brain biopsy.

2.20   C: Dextroamphetamine

This individual has narcolepsy (the sudden irresistible urge to sleep) and cataplexy (sudden loss of muscle tone following strong emotions or excitement). Cataplexy is seen in up to 70% of patients with narcolepsy, either at diagnosis or later in the disease. In narcolepsy, REM sleep occurs within 15 minutes in most subjects. Sleepiness is the main problem here, so treatment with stimulant drugs (amphetamine) to heighten alertness is most appropriate; however, imipramine may also be useful for cataplexy.

NEUROLOGY: MULITIPLE CHOICE ANSWERS

2.21   A C D E

CJD is a spongiform encephalopathy which usually presents as presenile dementia. 10–15% of cases are familial and onset is usually after the age of 50. Unsteadiness, memory and visual disturbance often occur early with progressive dementia, ataxia and upper motor neurone signs following. Myoclonus and aphasia may occur. CSF is usually normal and the EEG often shows periodic triphasic sharp waves. There is atrophy of most of the cortex with frontal, parietal and occipital lobes and cerebellum being worst affected. Recently a subgroup of CJD has been reported in much younger patients where psychiatric symptoms predominate early, leading to motor problems. There seem to be no characteristic EEG changes.

2.22   A C D E

Oligoclonal bands in the serum would suggest immunoglobulin production outside the CSF. Typically, visual evoked potentials are delayed (due to demyelination). Axonal loss would cause a decrease in amplitude. Prognosis is better in women and if the disease starts with optic or sensory symptoms. Increased age, progressive disease, spinal cord or cerebellar disease carry a poorer prognosis. Interferon has been shown to decrease the number and severity of relapses. Although some neurologists are sceptical of the trials these are the reasons why the drug has been given a licence in the UK.

2.23   B C E

The classic clinical triad of NPH is dementia with early urinary incontinence and gait disturbance. Patients with NPH may not have these features but the CT scan appearance is often helpful since hydrocephalus is present with an enlarged fourth ventricle but normal or compressed cortical sulci (i.e. the pattern of communicating hydrocephalus). Many patients improve with ventricular shunting though prior CSF flow studies may be necessary to identify patients most likely to improve. If hydrocephalus is present with a normal sized fourth ventricle then the diagnosis is likely to be aqueduct stenosis or other obstructive lesion between the fourth and third ventricle. Papilloedema is not a feature of NPH.

2.24   A B C D E

In pyramidal weakness the flexors are usually stronger than the extensors in the upper limbs and the reverse in the lower limbs. Hip flexion is often weaker than ankle dorsiflexion which in turn is weaker than knee flexion. Ankle clonus and ankle jerks use the same L5 / S1 reflex pathway. Motor neurone disease, hereditary spastic paraparesis and parasagital meningiomas may all cause pyramidal weakness without sensory signs.

2.25   A B D E

Some patients have vague sensory symptoms in the early stages of MND and limb pain is a surprisingly frequent problem later in the disease. However sensory signs are never present. Essential to the diagnosis is the demonstration that the peripheral sensory conduction velocities are normal. The glossopharyngeal nerve is purely sensory and so is not affected in MND, thus severe bulbar problems may be present, but palatal sensation is normal. The prognosis for life in MND once bulbar symptoms develop is usually measured in months. The abdominal reflexes, which usually disappear in the face of upper motor neurone lesions, are often strangely preserved in MND, the explanation is unknown.

2.26   B D E

The somatotopic arrangement in the spinothalamic tract has the lower spinal roots more lateral. The anterior spinal artery supplies the anterior two-thirds of the cord including the spinothalamic tracts. Syringomyelia, ependymomas and central astrocytomas will all cause a central cord syndrome.

2.27   C D E

Lesions in one or other cerebellar hemisphere usually cause peripheral limb ataxia (e.g. 'finger to nose ataxia') rather than ataxia of gait which is a feature of central cerebellar (vermis) lesions. Gait ataxia is associated with normal pressure hydrocephalus not benign intracranial hypertension. Cerebellar ectopia may present with a combination of gait ataxia and nystagmus (often downbeating vertically). Gait ataxia and other cerebellar signs are features of alcohol and anticonvulsant (including carbamazepine) toxicity.

2.28   A D

Tinel's sign is positive when tapping the wrist causes paraesthesia in the digits supplied by the median nerve. It is a sign of the carpal tunnel syndrome. Only three of the muscles of the thenar eminence are supplied by the median nerve, the abductor pollicis brevis, opponens pollicis and the flexor pollicis brevis. Prolongation of the latency of the sensory action potential is electrophysiological evidence of median nerve compression at the wrist, with progressive reduction of its amplitude as denervation occurs. Similarly the distal motor latency to median supplied muscles (abductor pollicis brevis is usually tested) is delayed in the face of normal motor conduction proximal to the wrist.

2.29   B C E

Drug toxicity (for example with phenytoin) may cause nystagmus in all directions, horizontal and vertical. If the fast phase is downbeating the lesion is usually low in the medulla near the cervico-medullary junction. Masses at this site (or the congenital Arnold-Chiari malformation) may present with a combination of occipital pain, ataxia and downbeating nystagmus. There may or may not be an oscillopsia, a sensation of the visual field bouncing up and down, with the nystagmus. Nystagmus does not occur in unconscious patients since the fast phase appears to depend on intact hemisphere function. In an unconscious patient with a thalamic lesion the eyes may be deviated downwards.

2.30   A B C

Triplet repeats have been shown as the genetic abnormality in a number of diseases. The number of repeats increases with sub-sequent generations and is thought to be the mechanism underlying 'anticipation' where succeeding generations inherit a more severe form of the disease. Gerstmann's syndrome occurs in some patients with parietal lobe damage (confusion between right and left limbs, finger agnosia, acalculia and agraphia).

2.31   B C D

Focal delta wave activity, particularly if continuous, suggests the presence of a structural brain lesion, but is pathologically non-specific and may occur after substantial vascular lesions of any type, tumours or even advanced neurodegenerative disease. Neurophysiologically this abnormality represents an area of electrically inactive cortex which allows the appearance on the surface EEG of underlying slow waves probably originating from the thalamic rhythm generators. The appearance of focal delta wave activity is an indication for further investigation by CT scanning. Although seizures may occur with such structural lesions the EEG appearances are not synonymous with clinical seizures, focal slow waves being seen in many patients with comparable structural lesions who have not had seizures.

2.32   B C D E

The tremor of Parkinson's disease is characteristically a rest tremor, though a mild action tremor is sometimes seen. Action tremors are usually an exaggeration of the normal physiological tremor, and like many tremors are worsened by anxiety. A marked action tremor may run in families and is seldom suggestive of serious neurological disease. Titubation of the head which is common in the elderly, is an action tremor of the neck muscles, is not a sign of Parkinson's disease and is usually benign but sometimes related to lesions of the superior cerebellar peduncle. The drug of first choice for troublesome action tremors is propranolol but in patients in whom this drug is ineffective or contraindicated, low doses of primidone may be effective.

2.33   B C E

Up to the first 12 hours or so after even a substantial cerebral infarction the CT scan may show very little change. In fact the extent of the low attenuation area caused by an infarction usually does not become clear for at least 12 hours and sometimes longer. Over the first 24–36 hours the ischaemic tissue swells, producing a mass effect on the scan by the second or third day which then subsides by the first week. Towards the end of the first week the infarcted tissue is invaded by phagocytic glial cells which may increase the X-ray attenuation of the area so that the plain scan looks (near) normal. However the infarct is also invaded by new blood vessels which show as areas of enhancement after injection of iodinated contrast medium. This post-contrast enhancement is maximal during the second week after the infarction. Carotid angiography after cerebral infarction may be normal even after substantial infarction. This occurs particularly following embolism when the causative occlusion may disperse. In such cases the longer after the stroke the angiogram is performed the more likely it is to be normal.

2.34   A C D

Hypothalamic damage frequently occurs after substantial SAH due to berry aneurysms. This causes excessive ADH secretion and is probably the cause of the surge of catecholamines which may cause life-threatening cardiac arrhythmias and subendocardial myocardial necrosis. There is usually a delay of some days (with a peak incidence in the second week) after SAH before secondary ischaemic changes become apparent. The risk of rebleeding, compared with deterioration due to vasospasm, has probably been overestimated and falls fairly sharply from up to 50% within the first month (in unoperated patients) such that at six months it is 3% per year. In general neurosurgeons do not consider aneurysmal clipping in patients who are unconscious since the outlook for such patients is so poor. Referral for such surgery is therefore delayed until the clinical condition of the patient has improved (provided that the diagnosis is clear).

2.35   A E

Despite raised pressure causing papilloedema BIH is a syndrome in which consciousness is clear and there are no focal neurological signs (although false localising signs such as sixth nerve palsies may occur). It may present with headache and transient visual obscurations which forewarn of visual failure. The cerebral ventricles are normal or smaller than usual, i.e. hydrocephalus is not present. BIH is not a feature of anorexia nervosa but occurs in young obese females often with menstrual irregularities. Other causes include pregnancy, the contraceptive pill, hypocortisolism, hypoparathyroidism, hyper- and hypovitaminosis A, tetracycline therapy and other drugs. Usually BIH is a self-limiting condition but because of the risk of visual loss, treatment with repeated lumbar puncture is advised. Steroids and carbonic anhydrase inhibitors have been suggested but are not usually effective.

2.36   A B D

Note the question asks for good prognostic indicators not indicators of a good prognosis! Low coma scale, skull fracture and absent somatosensory evoked responses are all good indicators of a poor prognosis.

2.37   A B C E

Trigeminal neuralgia, whilst usually idiopathic may be secondary to demyelination (in the pons), in which case trigger spots are rare and treatment is often ineffective. Phenytoin, carbamazepine and clonazepam are the usual medical treatments. There is no association with causalgia except the pain mechanism may be similar. Root or root entry zone compression may occur due to tumours or arteries.

2.38   B C D

Central pontine myelinolysis (CPM) occurs when there is demyelination of the pons or parapontine white matter. It is due to metabolic insults and is seen in alcoholics, leukaemia, hyperemesis gravidarum and other causes of prolonged vomiting. It is therefore associated with Wernicke's. A flaccid paralysis and eye movement disorders are common findings. Recovery depends on the treatment of the underlying disease and relapse of CPM does not occur unless there is relapse of the underlying cause.

2.39   B C

There are many paraneoplastic syndromes. Cerebellar degeneration is associated with anti-Purkinje cell antibodies (secondary to breast and ovary tumours). Vitamin E deficiency does cause a cerebellar degeneration but this is not paraneoplastic. Optic atrophy is secondary to retinal degeneration in this case. SIADH is due to an ADH like peptide release from the tumour and Cushing's syndrome, whatever the cause, may have a myopathy.

2.40   C

The twelfth cranial nerve or hypoglossal nerve innervates the musculature of the tongue. Paralysis of this musculature on one side causes the protruded tongue to be pushed over towards the weak side. The soft palate obtains its sensory innervation from the ninth (glossopharyngeal) cranial nerve and its motor innervation from the (tenth nerve) vagus. A combination of lesions on one side of cranial nerves 9, 10, 11 and 12 suggests that the lesion is at the jugular foramen just outside the skull, for example a glomus tumour. Taste over the anterior two-thirds of the tongue is supplied by fibres which run in the facial nerve.

2.41   B D E

The dorsal root ganglia of the spinal roots are in the exit foramina of the spine. Compression by an intervertebral disc usually occurs proximal to this site and therefore the sensory action potential in the distal neurone is intact. Nerve root compression often causes pain which is felt in the muscles supplied by that segment, for example in the pectoralis muscle and triceps in a C7 root compression. Compression in the lumbar region cannot cause upper motor signs since the spinal cord ends at L1. A large central disc in the lower lumbar region may compress the sacral roots in the cauda equina and cause bladder symptoms. The root innervation of the ankle reflex is S1 so compression of this root will cause loss of the ankle jerk.

2.42   C D

Sumatriptan affects blood flow by decreasing cerebral vasodilatation. It may be given at any stage of a migraine but should be avoided in combination with ergot, which still has a small part to play in management. Methysergide may cause retroperitoneal fibrosis and patients should be free from it for at least 3 months a year.

2.43   C D

The pathogenic mechanism in myasthenia gravis is the production of autoantibodies directed against the acetylcholine receptors on the motor end plate. These are present in 90% of patients with myasthenia although their titre correlates poorly with the clinical severity of the disease. Myasthenia in younger women is usually not associated with thymoma and responds well to thymectomy (some have recommended this as the first line of therapy in patients fit for operation). Older men with myasthenia are most likely to have a thymoma: it is present in about 10% of patients. Thymectomy is advised for such patients with thymoma because of the risks of local tumour infiltration but it usually has a disappointing effect on the myasthenia. Aminoglycoside antibiotics can worsen neuromuscular transmission in patients with myasthenia and may provoke onset. Pharmacological therapy of myasthenia is with long-acting anticholinesterase inhibitors, neostigmine and pyridostigmine. Edrophonium is too short acting for therapeutic use and is reserved for diagnostic purposes only.

2.44 A B D E

The unilateral lower motor neurone palsy of unknown origin known as Bell's palsy is often preceded by pain in the mastoid region. At least 80% of cases show complete recovery but total paralysis at onset is a poor prognostic sign. In the latter case recovery does occur but cross re-inervation may produce unsatisfactory results. Tarsorrhaphy to protect the cornea is hardly ever necessary in Bell's palsy, though a supply of artificial tears (hydroxymellose drops) may be necessary. Corneal sensation is always intact and the uprolling of the eye to blink (the Bell's phenomenon) is usually sufficient protection of the cornea before spontaneous recovery occurs. After about three weeks, if recovery has not occurred EMG tests may help predict prognosis. If there is no evidence of denervation the prognosis for recovery is good.

2.45 A D

A single seizure does not constitute epilepsy. However, there is a 40–80% chance of a further seizure within 12 months. An EEG within 24 hours of a fit will show non-specific slowing. A normal EEG does not exclude the diagnosis of epilepsy nor does a normal CT exclude the possibility of a structural (e.g. small CVA) cause. After a single unprovoked seizure driving is banned for one year. If more than one fit occurs driving is banned for one year after the last fit whether the patient is on or off treatment. If all seizures occur during sleep (during sleep not just at night!) and that pattern has been set for three years driving is allowed. The commonest cause of epilepsy in adult life is cerebrovascular disease.

PSYCHIATRY: 'BEST OF FIVE' ANSWERS

3.1   D: Lofexidine

Lofexidine is the drug of choice for treating opiate withdrawals. It is a central α_2 agonist and helps alleviate the symptoms of opiate withdrawal. A reducing regime of methadone can also be used to help withdraw from opiates. Diamorphine for the treatment of addiction can only be prescribed by doctors specifically licensed to prescribe to addicts. Benzodiazepines and neuroleptics can help relieve symptoms, but are not as effective as lofexidine. Bupropion is a noradrenaline and dopamine reuptake inhibitor and is prescribed as an aid to smoking cessation.

3.2   C: Primary delusion

All of the options listed are features of schizophrenia. A delusion is a false, unshakable belief out of keeping with a patient's social and cultural background. Primary delusions appear suddenly and with full conviction. Delusional perceptions are examples of primary delusions and are of first rank importance in the diagnosis of schizophrenia. A delusional perception occurs when an individual forms an instantaneous delusion after a normal perception, for example suddenly believing he is Jesus on seeing a blue car drive past. A secondary delusion is derived from an abnormal mental phenomenon, for example believing one is Jesus because the hallucinatory voice of God has told him so. Other first rank symptoms are audible thoughts, third person auditory hallucinations, passivity and thought broadcasting, insertion or withdrawal.

3.3   E: Self-induced vomiting

The most important feature of anorexia nervosa is that low weight is self-induced. This may be by the restriction of "fattening foods" from the diet, self-induced vomiting or purging, excessive exercising or the use of appetite suppressants or diuretics. Body image is distorted, with sufferers not accepting they are underweight. There is also a widespread endocrine disturbance producing a number of symptoms including amenorrhoea in women. Appetite is usually present but consciously suppressed. The BMI is calculated by dividing weight in Kg by height in M squared (kg/m^2) and in anorexia is 17.5 or less. Lower BMIs could also be as a result of starvation from other causes.

3.4   A: Cognitive behavioural therapy

The patient described has features of clinical depression. Key diagnostic features are depressed mood, increased fatigability and anhedonia (loss of interest and enjoyment). Trials of different kinds of psychotherapy are difficult to conduct. However, for cases of mild to moderate depression, cognitive-behavioural therapy (CBT) has been shown to be as effective as antidepressants.

3.5   A: Anxiety in crowded places

Agoraphobia is defined as a fear of the related aspects of open spaces. This would include the presence of crowds and difficulty escaping to a safe place – usually home. This fear characteristically leads to avoidance of the phobic situation, hence a possible reason for poor attendance in clinic. Anxiety and panic attacks in agoraphobia are predictable and linked to the phobic situation. Unpredictable panic attacks are part of panic disorder. Anxiety predominant in social situations occurs in social phobia.

3.6   E: Thought alienation

Thought alienation is a disorder of the possession of thought. The individual has the experience that his thoughts are under the control of an outside person or force. Examples of thought alienation include thought withdrawal, thought insertion and thought broadcasting. Hallucinations are perceptions experienced without any external stimulus. Hallucinations heard when going to sleep (hypnagogic) or on waking (hypnopompic) can occur in tired, healthy people and in sleep disorders such as narcolepsy. Depersonalisation occurs when a person feels numb and unreal. Derealisation occurs when his environment feels unreal. Both states are unpleasant and occur in a large number of psychiatric disorders, especially anxiety states, depression and schizophrenia. They can also occur in tired, healthy individuals.

3.7   A: Amphetamine

Amphetamines can produce a schizophrenia-like illness in otherwise healthy individuals. Cannabis is thought to bring on schizophrenia early in susceptible individuals, but is otherwise unlikely to produce a schizophreniform psychosis. LSD and psilocybin (found in magic mushrooms) produce perceptual abnormalities mainly during intoxication, but do not produce first rank schizophrenic symptoms. Heroin use does not produce psychotic symptoms.

3.8   A: Inability to feel sadness

Uncomplicated grief reactions consist of three stages. The first stage should only last a maximum of a few days and is characterised by denial and numbness. The second stage can last up to six months or one year. This stage is characterised by intense sadness, loneliness, yearning for the dead person, anorexia, poor sleep and anxiety. Fleeting hallucinations of the dead person may also occur. In the third stage symptoms subside and there is gradual acceptance and readjustment. Pathological grief consists of a delayed, inhibited or abnormally long period of grieving. There may also be a typical depressive picture with marked feelings of worthlessness, psychomotor retardation or functional impairment.

3.9   D: Intrusive flashbacks

Repeated reliving of trauma through flashbacks (intrusive memories) or nightmares is typical, with avoidance of situations that might trigger painful memories. The traumatic event must be exceptionally violent or catastrophic in nature. There is often accompanying autonomic hyperarousal, emotional blunting, anhedonia and other features of anxiety and depression, but these are not essential to make the diagnosis. Believing his attackers have followed him to the UK is suggestive of a persecutory delusion, which is not typical of PTSD.

3.10   A: Global memory loss

Patients with depressive pseudodementia are often detailed historians, but perform badly on tests of cognitive functioning. Patients with dementia often demonstrate recent memory loss, whereas those with depression complain of global memory loss. Both groups may have poor concentration, but patients with dementia often make more of an effort with testing. Parietal lobe abnormalities such as dyspraxias or topographical disorientation should not occur in depression.

3.11   E: Somatisation disorder

Somatisation disorder is characterised by multiple, changing physical symptoms that have been present for at least two years. As a result of the symptoms, the patient's life becomes considerably disrupted. However the patient refuses to accept reassurance from negative test results and medical opinion. In hypochondriacal disorder the patient's focus is not on the symptoms, but on the presence of an underlying serious disease such as cancer or cardiovascular disease. The terms dissociative (psychiatric) and conversion (physical) disorder have replaced the old-fashioned, imprecise term hysteria. (see questions 18 & 23).

3.12   B: Intellectual deterioration

Approximately 60% of sufferers with multiple sclerosis demonstrate a degree of intellectual deterioration. This can vary from mild memory loss to profound global dementia. Fleeting mood disorders are very common, with major depressive episodes occurring in approximately half of sufferers. Euphoria occurs in about 10% and is commonly associated with severe cognitive impairment. Psychotic episodes are rare.

3.13   D: Korsakoff's syndrome

Hyperemesis can result in acute thiamine deficiency and subsequent Wernicke's encephalopathy. The majority of cases then progress to Korsakoff's psychosis, a type of amnesic syndrome. Characteristic features of amnesic syndrome include temporal disorientation and very poor retention of recent memories. This is tested by immediate and 5 minute recall. Registration of new information will be intact, but recall several minutes later will be impaired. Confabulation can also occur, where detailed memories are recalled which turn out to be inaccurate.

3.14   E: Negativism

Schizophrenic symptoms can be divided into positive and negative. Positive symptoms often occur in acute episodes and include hallucinations, delusions, formal thought disorder and bizarre behaviour. Negative symptoms are associated with a more chronic picture and may be very disabling. These symptoms include poverty of speech (alogia), poor motivation and initiative (avolition), an inability to derive pleasure from activities (anhedonia), emotional blunting and attentional deficits. Catatonia can occur in schizophrenia and is a disorder of psychomotor activity. Symptoms include stupor, excitement, waxy flexibility, mutism and negativism.

3.15   C: Perseverating responses

Frontal lobe dysfunction can result in personality changes, disinhibition and euphoria, or apathy and slowing of thought and motor activity. Perseveration of actions and difficulties in planning and executing actions can also occur. Impaired five-minute recall can suggest bilateral temporal lobe dysfunction. Sensory dysphasia can occur if the dominant temporal lobe is affected. Right-left disorientation is part of Gerstmann's syndrome, affecting the dominant parietal lobe. Hypersomnia may result from dysfunction of the diencephalon and brainstem.

3.16   B: Obsessive compulsive disorder

A number of psychiatric and physical illnesses are associated with increased risk of suicide. Despite high rates of morbidity and considerably impaired functioning, the suicide rate in obsessive compulsive disorder (OCD) is considerably lower than in depressed patients without OCD.

3.17   D: IM Lorazepam

In a patient who is neuroleptic naïve, antipsychotics should be administered with caution. Parenteral administration should be avoided if possible until the response to an oral dose has been assessed. Reasons include an increased risk of cardiovascular complications when antipsychotics are administered parenterally to highly agitated individuals. There is also the risk of acute dystonic reactions. Chlorpromazine in addition is highly irritant when administered IM. Benzodiazepines, often followed by oral antipsychotics, are generally a safer option in this situation. IM diazepam however is poorly absorbed.

3.18   C: Fluctuating recall

Dissociative disorders are examples of "psychogenic" disorders which do not have sufficient evidence of a physical disorder to explain the symptoms. In dissociative amnesia there is a persistent core of amnesia, which cannot be recalled. However the extent and completeness of amnesia varies from day to day and between investigators. The accompanying affect can vary from distress with attention seeking to calm acceptance. Disorientation or disturbances of consciousness or awareness would indicate organic disorder.

3.19   B: Sentences spoken are connected by clanging

Thought disorder occurs when there is a loss of the normal, logical progression of thinking. There are a number of types of schizophrenic thought disorder including derailment (A), incoherence (B) and illogicality. In mania thought disorder can occur in the form of flight of ideas. Thoughts follow each other rapidly, with the connection between them often based on verbal associations such as rhyming, alliteration or clanging e.g. "My car is a rover. Rover is a great dog. Fancy a snog?"

3.20   A: Acknowledging this belief is irrational, but still refusing

Obsessional thoughts often involve contamination as a theme. They may involve an accompanying compulsive act or ritual that lessens the anxiety associated with the thought. The ritual itself is not inherently pleasurable. Obsessional thoughts must be recognised as the individual's own thoughts and are therefore not part of a psychotic process. The thoughts are commonly perceived as being senseless and are resisted, but at a cost of considerable anxiety.

3.21   E: Short-term memory loss

All of the above sequelae can occur after a head injury. However, short-term memory loss is usually the most persistent cognitive dysfunction. Focal brain pathology after a head injury can result in focal deficits. For example executive dysfunction, including the impaired planning and executing of actions, can occur with frontal lobe pathology.

3.22   A: Ataxia

The answer to this question is ataxia as you have been asked which abnormality is most likely to indicate toxicity. Tremor can occur at therapeutic plasma levels, whereas ataxia should only occur in toxicity. Lithium has a low therapeutic index, but can produce a number of unpleasant side-effects at therapeutic levels (0.4–1.1 meq/l). These include fine tremor, nausea, vomiting, diarrhoea and metallic taste. A coarse tremor, ataxia, slurred speech, disorientation and convulsions can occur in toxicity.

3.23   C: Fasciculations

Conversion disorders frequently present to doctors. They are characterised by the presence of symptoms or deficits involving voluntary motor or sensory functions. In motor conversion disorders, the patient may not be able to contract a particular muscle group. However tests often show that the muscles are able to contract when the patient's attention is diverted. Changes in reflexes are not present, but disuse atrophy can occur in chronic cases.

3.24   E: The majority of cases are preceded by anorexia nervosa

To make a diagnosis of bulimia nervosa there must be recurrent episodes of binge eating – eating larger than normal amounts of food accompanied by a loss of control over eating. In addition there must be recurrent compensatory behaviour to prevent weight gain e.g. self-induced vomiting, laxative or diuretic abuse, fasting or excessive exercising. A fear of fatness is also prominent. About 1/3 of patients with bulimia may previously have had anorexia nervosa. If all features are present apart from compensatory behaviour, the condition is known as binge-eating disorder.

3.25   E: Hallucinations must occur in clear consciousness

Alcoholic hallucinosis is characterised by second person auditory hallucinations of a derogatory or persecutory nature. Hallucinations occur in clear consciousness and are therefore not part of a delirium or other acute withdrawal syndrome. Hallucinations lasting beyond six months generally develop into either a schizophrenic or amnesic syndrome.

PSYCHIATRY: MULTIPLE CHOICE ANSWERS

3.26   B C D E

Fragile X syndrome has been recognised in recent years as the commonest cause of X-linked mental retardation. The cardinal features are male sex, facial abnormalities (bat ears, large jaw, maxillary hypoplasia) macro-orchidism and a marker (an apparent gap in the long arm of the X-chromosome) in lymphocytic culture under reducing conditions. This marker can be seen in amniotic fluid cells and therefore prenatal diagnosis is possible. Carrier females are usually of normal intelligence, but about 10% have mild mental retardation. Recent reports have suggested high rates of infantile autism and hyperkinetic syndrome.

3.27   E

CNS involvement occurs in about one-third of cases of SLE. Psychiatric symptoms occur in 60% of cases: the excess is due to both psychological reactions to illness and corticosteroid side effects. The commonest presentations are acute organic states and neurotic disorders; schizophrenia-like syndromes are rare. Mental symptoms are seldom the first signs of SLE (which are usually fever, malaise and arthralgia). When present, psychiatric symptoms often fluctuate, usually remit within six weeks but may recur. The presence of cerebral vasculitis substantially worsens prognosis.

3.28   A B

Most mental retardation is of uncertain aetiology. In mild retardation (IQ less than 50) there is a strong association with social handicap and low IQ in the family. Therefore, many cases represent the lower end of the intelligence spectrum ('subcultural' retardation). All psychiatric disorders are more common in mental retardation, although diagnosis is often difficult. Phenylketonuria requires dietary phenylalanine exclusion which can probably be ended after adolescence. Cretinism (congenital hypothyroidism) is not clinically detectable until six months. Lesch-Nyhan syndrome is an X-linked syndrome producing choreoathetoid movements and self mutilation. Neurofibromatosis is an autosomal dominant inherited disorder characterised by multiple tumours and vitiligo which only produces intellectual retardation in a minority of cases.

3.29   C D E

Family studies have shown that first degree relatives of schizophrenics have an increased rate of schizophrenia themselves (5–12% compared to 1% in the general population). Twin and adoption studies have confirmed the genetic contribution to aetiology. However twins *per se* have no greater risk than non-twins. Relatives also have higher rates of personality disorder and alcoholism but not depression or organic psychosis. Familial risk is less in late onset cases.

3.30   A B D E

Seven essential elements in the alcohol dependence syndrome have been described. These include a compulsion to drink (and continue drinking), primacy of drinking over other activities, an altered tolerance to alcohol, repeated withdrawal symptoms, drinking to relieve withdrawal (and particularly early morning drinking) and reinstatement after abstinence. The final element, a stereotyped pattern of drinking, refers to an unvarying daily pattern of drinking at regular intervals in order to ward off withdrawal symptoms. Whilst alcoholics often progress to stronger and cheaper sources of alcohol this is not an essential element of the syndrome.

3.31   A B C D

Acute mania is treated with a neuroleptic such as chlorpromazine. Immediate sedation is superseded by an antimanic effect over some weeks. Additional short-term sedation with a benzodiazepine is sometimes required. Lithium is an antimanic agent with a similar latency of action and less efficacy than neuroleptics. It is sometimes used to augment the neuroleptic effect but occasional neurotoxicity has been reported. Carbamazepine has a mild antimanic effect but is used primarily as a prophylactic agent in patients intolerant to lithium or who have rapid cycling disorders (more than three episodes per year). ECT still has a role in drug-resistant manic patients. Procyclidine is used to treat the Parkinsonian side-effects of neuroleptics.

3.32   A C D E

DTs are the most serious of the alcohol withdrawal phenomenon with a mortality of up to 5%. Prodromal symptoms occur shortly after abstinence but the full blown syndrome, characterised by vivid hallucinations, occurs 3–4 days later. Illusions and hallucinations are primarily visual but auditory and haptic hallucinations also occur. Lilliputian hallucinations may be accompanied by amusement and jocularity but an effect of apprehension and fear is more typical. Other symptoms include delusions, confusion, inattention, agitation, restlessness, tremor, autonomic overactivity and sleeplessness. Biochemical abnormalities include hypomagnesaemia, hypokalaemia and hypoglycaemia. Treatment is primarily with sedation, using chlordiazepoxide or chlormethiazole, adequate hydration, vitamin supplementation and anticonvulsant cover where there is a history of seizure.

3.33   D

Tardive dyskinesia is characterised by chewing, sucking and grimacing of the face and choreoathetoid movements. It occurs in about one-fifth of patients receiving long-term treatment with neuroleptic medication such as phenothiazines or butyrophenones. Increased incidence is seen with females and increasing age but not brain damage or previous treatment with ECT. Few treatments are helpful and stopping the offending drug may produce paradoxical worsening. There is decreased life expectancy when functional psychosis and severe dyskinesia are both present.

3.34   A B C D

Hospital surveys have emphasised the frequency of psychiatric illness on general medical wards. The most common reason for admission is a drug overdose. Among patients admitted for other reasons, depression (10–25%) and alcohol abuse (15–30%) are very common. The diagnosis is often missed, especially if tearfulness or behaviour disturbances are not evident. This is important as continued psychiatric symptoms delay medical recovery. Research has shown that medical students can detect psychiatric cases more readily than house officers or ward nurses. About 10% of deliberate self-harm patients need inpatient psychiatric treatment.

3.35   D E

Recent double blind trials have confirmed the particular value of electroconvulsive therapy in depression especially when endogenous features or delusions are present. Although less used in other conditions, it is of value in neurotic depression, mania and schizophrenia. It causes brief memory disturbances after each application, especially when bilateral rather than unilateral electrodes are used. However, there is little evidence that permanent memory deficits occur. Age is no contraindication to treatment.

3.36   E

Serious and minor mental disorders are considerably more common in the postpartum period. 'Maternity blues' is a self-limiting episode of mood lability occurring in about half of new mothers. Puerperal psychosis is far less common. No specific causative factors are known. A variety of presentations are possible, including acute organic reactions with clouding of consciousness. The development of supervised mother-and-baby units within psychiatric hospitals has avoided the need for separation and the consequent disruption of emotional 'bonding'. Psychosis recurs in about 20% of later pregnancies.

3.37   B D E

In endogenous depression, there is persistent depression of mood, unreactive to circumstances. Characteristic symptoms include early morning waking, morning worsening of mood, feelings of guilt or worthlessness with decline in concentration, energy, appetite, interest and libido. Although tricyclic antidepressants and electroconvulsive therapy (ECT) are the treatments of choice, some cases, especially when agitation and/or delusions are present, respond to chlor-promazine alone. Affective incongruity is a feature of schizophrenia.

3.38   A B C D E

Suicide is commonest amongst elderly men, although rates amongst young men have been rising dramatically in recent years. Rates increase progressively through the married, never married, widowers and widows and the divorced. Suicide is increased amongst social classes I and V, individuals with a past history of suicide attempts, history of depression, alcohol abuse, drug abuse, schizophrenia or antisocial or borderline personality disorders. Feelings of hopelessness are an important predictor of immediate and long-term suicide risk. In most cases a warning is given before committing suicide with 2/3 expressing suicidal ideas to relatives and 1/3 expressing clear suicidal intent. 40% of suicide completers had consulted their GP in the previous week.

3.39   A D

Anorexia nervosa is defined by self-induced weight loss, abnormal attitudes to food and body weight and amenorrhoea in women or loss of libido in men. There are many endocrine changes e.g. raised cortisol and growth hormone, and decreased gonadotrophins. However there is little evidence that it is a primary endocrinological disorder. Structural lesions are rarely discovered. Clinical features include lanugo, a type of downy hair found on the extremities. Induced vomiting and purging to reduce weight often result in hypokalaemia.

3.40   C D

Panic attacks are characterised by a sudden onset of extreme fear, an impending feeling of doom and somatic symptoms including tachycardia, palpitations, dyspnoea and sweating. Usually no precipitant is evident and attacks last 20–30 minutes. As many as 50% of patients have prolapse of one of the mitral valve leaflets, resulting in a midsystolic click on cardiac auscultation. The mainstay of treatment is antidepressants. Behavioural treatments may help with residual anxiety symptoms although controlled breathing and breathing into a bag are sometimes useful for attacks. Social phobia is a persistent fear of social appraisal and is not directly linked to panic disorder although most cases of agoraphobia are thought to be secondary to it.

3.41   A B C E

Delirium is an acute onset syndrome characterised by inattention and an impaired level of consciousness. Thinking is often disorganised and perseverative. Perceptual disturbances include misinterpretations, illusions and hallucinations. There is disturbance of the sleep-wake cycle with insomnia and daytime sleepiness. Psychomotor activity may be increased or decreased. Disorientation and memory impairment are common. The patient has no insight during episodes of confusion and amnesia for the episode once it has resolved. A catastrophic reaction has been described in dementing patients which is characterised by marked agitation secondary to the subjective awareness of intellectual deficits under stressful circumstances.

3.42   B C

Treatment of schizophrenia is with long-term neuroleptic medication, often in depot form to ensure compliance. 70% respond to conventional neuroleptics and of the remainder 50% respond to the atypical antipsychotic clozapine. Patients taking clozapine require regular blood monitoring in view of the risk of neutropenia and potentially fatal agranulocytosis. Family therapy may reduce relapse if relatives show high levels of 'expressed emotion'. Cognitive behavioural therapy may help patients with chronic symptoms and possibly also in the acute stages of the illness. Psychodynamic therapy is not useful and may precipitate a relapse in some patients. Psychosurgery is rarely used in intractable cases of depression and obsessive-compulsive disorder but has no role in the treatment of schizophrenia.

3.43   A D E

Postural hypotension is a serious side-effect of tricyclic antidepressants, particularly in the elderly. Typical antipsychotics such as haloperidol have an antipsychotic action which is proportional to their antagonism of the dopamine D2 receptor. Tranylcypromine is a reversible inhibitor of MAO with some amphetamine-like properties. Ingestion of vasoactive amines, such as tyramine in cheese, may lead to a hyperadrenergic crisis. 50–70% of patients on long-term lithium develop polyuria, with 10% having an output exceeding 3 litres per day, thus qualifying as having nephrogenic diabetes insipidus. Lithium also inhibits adenylyl cyclase activation by TSH which is thought to be a factor in the production of drug-induced hypothyroidism or goitre.

3.44   A B C

Neuroleptic malignant syndrome is an uncommon but increasingly recognised side effect of neuroleptic administration. The syndrome is characterised by hyperthermia, muscle rigidity, a fluctuant conscious level, features of sympathetic discharge and, less consistently, dystonias and dyskinesias. It occurs at therapeutic doses. The most frequently implicated drug is haloperidol. Tricyclic antidepressant therapy and L-dopa withdrawal are occasional causes. There is no specific treatment. A significant minority of cases are fatal; the rest recover after drug withdrawal within one to three weeks.

3.45   A B C D

SSRIs are effective antidepressants with less sedative effect than tricyclics, few antimuscarinic effects and low cardiotoxicity. The most frequent side-effects are gastrointestinal (diarrhoea, nausea and vomiting) which are dose related. Restlessness, anxiety, insomnia and sweating may be marked initially. Side-effects also include anorexia, weight loss and allergic reactions including anaphylaxis (all more common with fluoxetine), convulsions (particularly with fluvoxamine), extrapyramidal reactions and a withdrawal syndrome (particularly with paroxetine), abnormalities of hepatic enzymes (particularly with fluvoxamine and sertraline) and sexual dysfunction including anorgasmia and ejaculatory failure in males (particularly with paroxetine and fluoxetine).

3.46   B C D E

Studies report a significant increase in average lateral ventricle size in schizophrenics compared with normal controls, although with a marked overlap between the two populations. Third ventricle and cortical sulcal enlargement has also been reported. Medial temporal lobe structures appear reduced in volume, particularly on the left, and MRI has revealed widespread grey (but not white) matter volume deficits. Studies utilizing unaffected siblings as controls have demonstrated ventricular enlargement in the majority of patients. It has been demonstrated at illness onset and tends not to be progressive. There has been no consistent correlation shown between the degree of enlargement and symptoms although a relationship may exist with generalized cognitive deficits.

3.47   B C

The EEG in CJD initially shows diffuse or focal slowing which is nonspecific to this disorder. Later repetitive sharp waves or slow spike and wave discharges appear, which are bilaterally synchronous and may accompany myoclonic jerks. In the later stages of the disorder a characteristic pattern emerges of synchronous triphasic sharp wave complexes, superimposed on progressive suppression of cortical background activity. The sharp wave complexes become increasingly periodic at rates of one to two per second. These latter changes strongly suggest a diagnosis of CJD. Whilst EEG abnormalities found in epileptic patients are to some degree heritable those in CJD are not.

3.48   A B E

Factitious disorder is characterised by an intentional production of physical or psychological symptoms with an evident psychological need to assume the sick role. The disorder is best known as Münchausen's syndrome and patients are very difficult to manage, often discharging themselves when confronted with their factitious behaviour. In malingering there is an obvious, recognizable environmental goal in producing symptoms, beyond assuming the sick role. Somatization disorder is characterised by multiple physical complaints. Despite the absence of any physical disorder which would explain them the patient genuinely believes himself to be ill. Hysterical conversion disorders are characterised by physical, often neurological, symptoms which produce evident primary and secondary gain, but which are not consciously simulated by the patient.

3.49   C D

Huntington's chorea is an uncommon autosomal dominant disorder affecting 4–7 per 100,000 of the population. Senile and drug-induced choreas are much more frequently encountered. Anatomically, the frontal lobes and the caudate nucleus are most severely affected by neuronal loss and gliosis. Decreased concentrations of the inhibitory transmitter gamma-aminobutyric acid (GABA) and its enzyme glutamic acid decarboxylase (GAD) are usually detected. Dementia is usual although not invariable and progresses slowly over five to fifteen years.

3.50   A B E

Down's syndrome is the commonest known cause of moderate or severe subnormality (IQ less than 50). Characteristic features include small mouth with furrowed tongue and high palate, flat occiput, eyes with oblique palpebral fissures and epicanthic folds, hypotonia, short broad hands with curved little finger and a single palmar crease. Congenital heart disease (especially septal defects) occurs in one-fifth of cases. Behaviour disorders are less common than in many syndromes of mental handicap. Despite improvements in care, death in early or middle life is still usual.

REVISION CHECKLISTS

BASIC SCIENCES: REVISION CHECKLIST

Physiology

- [ ] Changes in pregnancy
- [ ] Haemoglobin function
- [ ] Physiology of bone
- [ ] Aetiology of oedema

Pathology

- [ ] Amyloid plaques

Hormone and mediator biochemistry

- [ ] Atrial natriuretic peptides
- [ ] Insulin/insulin resistance
- [ ] Adenosine
- [ ] ADH
- [ ] Aldosterone
- [ ] Angiotensin
- [ ] EDRF (nitric oxide)
- [ ] H_2 receptors
- [ ] Neurotransmitters
- [ ] Prostacyclin
- [ ] Somatostatin
- [ ] Steroid receptors

Miscellaneous

- [ ] Apolipoproteins
- [ ] Alpha$_1$-antitrypsin
- [ ] Mitochondrial DNA function
- [ ] Oncogenes

Abnormalities of brain & cerebral circulation

- ☐ Dementia/Alzheimer's
- ☐ Transient ischaemic attacks
- ☐ Benign intracranial hypertension/brain tumour
- ☐ Head injury
- ☐ Lateral medullary/circulatory syndromes
- ☐ Subdural haematoma
- ☐ Encephalitis
- ☐ Parietal lobe/frontal cortical lesions
- ☐ Temporal lobe epilepsy
- ☐ Amnesia
- ☐ Central pontine myelinolysis
- ☐ Cerebral abscess
- ☐ Creutzfeldt-Jakob disease
- ☐ EEG
- ☐ Intracranial calcification
- ☐ Midbrain (Parinaud's) syndrome
- ☐ Normal pressure hydrocephalus
- ☐ Wernicke's encephalopathy

Spinal cord and peripheral nerve anatomy & lesions

- ☐ Innervation of specific muscles
- ☐ Median nerve/brachial plexus
- ☐ Posterior nerve root/spinal ganglia lesions
- ☐ Dorsal interosseous nerve
- ☐ Guillain-Barré
- ☐ Pyramidal tracts/posterior column pathways
- ☐ Sciatic nerve lesion
- ☐ Autonomic spondylosis
- ☐ Cervical spondylosis
- ☐ Motor neurone disease
- ☐ Paraesthesia
- ☐ Spinal cord lesions

Cranial nerve anatomy & lesions

- ☐ Facial nerve
- ☐ Cranial nerve lesions
- ☐ Third nerve palsy/pupillary reflex
- ☐ Bulbar palsy
- ☐ Internuclear ophthalmoplegia
- ☐ 4th nerve palsy

Dyskinesias

- ☐ Ataxia
- ☐ Benign essential tremor
- ☐ Dyskinesia
- ☐ Parkinson's disease

Muscular disorders

- ☐ Duchenne muscular dystrophy
- ☐ Myotonic dystrophy
- ☐ Myaesthenia gravis

Miscellaneous

- ☐ Multiple sclerosis
- ☐ Headache/migraine
- ☐ Lumbar puncture/CSF
- ☐ Nystagmus
- ☐ Pseudofits
- ☐ Vertigo/dysarthria
- ☐ CNS involvement in AIDS

PSYCHIATRY: REVISION CHECKLIST

Psychotic disorders
- [ ] Schizophrenia
- [ ] Depression
- [ ] Mania
- [ ] Hallucinations/delusions

Anxiety states/compulsive disorders
- [ ] Neurosis/psychogenic/conversion disorders
- [ ] Obsessional/compulsive disorders
- [ ] Panic attack

Eating disorders
- [ ] Anorexia nervosa
- [ ] Bulimia

Other cognitive disorders
- [ ] Differentiation of dementia and depression
- [ ] Acute confusional state

Miscellaneous
- [ ] Psychiatric manifestations of organic disease
- [ ] Alcohol dependency
- [ ] Insomnia
- [ ] Narcolepsy
- [ ] Endocrine causes of psychiatric disease
- [ ] Psychiatric manifestations in adolescence

INDEX

Numbers refer to question numbers

Basic Sciences

Neurology

Psychiatry

PASTEST BOOKS FOR MRCP PART 1

MRCP 1 New Pocket Series
Further titles in this range:

Book 1:	Cardiology, Haematology, Respiratory	*1901198 758*
Book 2:	Basic Sciences, Neurology, Psychiatry	*1901198 804*
Book 3:	Endocrinology, Gastroenterology, Nephrology	*1901198 855*

MRCP 1 New 'Best of Five' Multiple Choice Revision Book
K Binymin   *1901198 57X*
Our new 'Best of Five' Multiple Choice Revision book features subject-based chapters ensuring all topics are fully covered. Practise new format 'best of five' questions to give confidence in your ability to sit the exam.

MRCP 1 Multiple True/False Revision Book
P Kalra   *1901198 952*
This book brings together 600 PasTest multiple true/false questions into one volume. The book is split into subjects but also contains a practice exam so that you can test your knowledge. Again, detailed teaching notes are provided.

Essential Revision Notes for MRCP Revised Edition
P Kalra   *1901198 596*
A definitive guide to revision for the MRCP examination. 19 chapters of informative material necessary to gain a successful exam result.

Explanations to the RCP 1997 and 1998 Past Papers
G Rees   *1901198 286*
360 answers and teaching notes to the Royal College of Physicians book of MCQs from the MRCP Part 1 1997 and 1998 Examinations.

Explanations to the RCP 1990 Past Papers
H Beynon & C Ross   *1901198 576*
180 answers and teaching notes to the Royal College of Physicians book of MCQs from the MRCP Part 1 1990 Examinations.

MRCP Part 1 MCQs with Key Topic Summaries 2nd edition
P O'Neill   *1901198 073*
200 MCQs with comprehensive key topic summaries bridging the gap between standard MCQ books and textbooks.

MRCP Part 1 MCQs in Basic Sciences
P Easterbrook & K Mokbel   *1901198 347*
300 exam-based MCQs focusing on basic sciences, with answers and teaching notes.